Learn Mexican Spanish Like Never Before!

Start Speaking Spanish Today with this Easy Step-By-Step Guide - Complete Beginner to Intermediate Level!

Jackson Bennett

© **Copyright 2025 - All rights reserved.**

The content contained within this book may not be reproduced, duplicated, or transmitted without direct written permission from the author or the publisher.

Under no circumstances will any blame or legal responsibility be held against the publisher or author for any damages, reparation, or monetary loss due to the information contained within this book, either directly or indirectly.

Legal Notice:

This book is copyright-protected. It is only for personal use. You cannot amend, distribute, sell, use, quote, or paraphrase any part or the content within this book without the consent of the author or publisher.

Disclaimer Notice:

Please note the information contained within this document is for educational and entertainment purposes only. All efforts have been executed to present accurate, up-to-date, reliable, and complete information. No warranties of any kind are declared or implied. Readers acknowledge that the author is not engaged in the rendering of legal, financial, medical, or professional advice. The content within this book has been derived from various sources. Please consult a licensed professional before attempting any techniques outlined in this book.

By reading this document, the reader agrees that under no circumstances is the author responsible for any losses, direct or indirect, that are incurred as a result of the use of the information contained within this document, including, but not limited to, errors, omissions, or inaccuracies.

Table of Contents

Introduction 1
The Alphabet (El Alfabeto) 3
    The Vowels (Las Vocales) 4
    The Consonants (Las Consonantes) 4
Syllables, Stress, and Accent Marks 14
    Syllables (Sílabas) 14
    Stress 17
    Accent Marks 18
Nouns 21
    The Gender of Living Nouns 21
    The Gender of Non-living Nouns 24
    Nouns that can be Both Genders 26
Plural Nouns 28
    Pluralizing Nouns 28
    Uncountable Nouns 29
Articles (A, an & the) 30
Numbers 36
    Cardinal Numbers 36
    Ordinal Numbers 42
    Time 47
    Days, Months & Dates 51
How to say I, You, He, She, etc. 56
Adjectives 57
Prepositions 72
    Common Prepositional Phrases Related to Place/Location 76
    The Fusion of Prepositions and Definite Articles 76
Verbs 82
    Conjugation 82
    Regular Verbs 83
    Irregular Verbs 89
    Stem-changing Verbs 101
Adverbs 105
    Adverbs of Manner 105
    Adverbs of Time 106
    Adverbs of Place 107
    Adverbs of Quantity 108
    Adverbs of Affirmation and Negation 108

- Adverbs of Doubt...109

The Gerund 111
Past Participles 113
- Forming Perfect Tenses..115
- Using as Adjectives..117
- Forming the Passive Voice...117

Reflexive Verbs 119
Sentences..121
- Declarative Sentences..122
- Negation Sentences..123
- Questions..125
- Indirect Questions...128
- Uses of 'Qué'..128
- Sentences involving Direct and Indirect Object Pronouns......................130
- Sentence Starters and Connectors...135

Vocabulary...141
- Titles and Relations..141
- Profession...143
- Endearment Terms...144
- Expressing Likes and Dislikes..144
- Love Expressions...150
- Movie Related..151
- Restaurant..151
- Ask/Request...152
- Giving Thanks..153
- Place and Building Names...154
- Directions...156
- Shopping..161
- Transportation..162
- Household Terms...165
- Electronics...169
- Food..170
- Clothes and Accessories...176
- Ornaments...177
- Colors..177
- Body..179
- Animals..181
- Versatile Words...182

Ways to Start a Conversation..186
Culture Insights..199

Slang Words 204
Do's and Don'ts in Mexico 204
Conclusion 206
Answers 207
References 224

Introduction

How many times have you felt frustrated while trying to learn a new language? The countless amount of time you have dedicated to it while feeling that you haven't improved a little can be very frustrating. I understand it very well. I also understand that learning a new language is not easy for everyone as there are so many options and methods out there, and it can become quite overwhelming.

This is why I decided to create this simple guide for you: to help you understand the language and develop the abilities that will help you expand your knowledge.

In this book, you will take a closer look at the alphabet and its sounds, explore grammar and vocabulary, learn to initiate conversation, and dive into cultural insights. You'll also discover useful slang, understand common expressions, and so much more. Each chapter is designed to help you gradually develop your skills through a combination of theory and practical exercises. All the answers can be found at the back of the book; however, please check them only after you have completed each exercise. By the end of this journey, you will not only be able to speak the language but also appreciate its rich cultural tapestry, ensuring that you feel truly confident and connected.

To begin, let's first take a moment to explore some fascinating history.

Mexico has been independent for over two hundred years. During this time, the country has experienced many changes in its culture, language, and society. Spanish wasn't the first language spoken in the territory. There were nearly five hundred Indigenous languages before the arrival of the Spaniards. After the Spanish conquered the Aztec Empire, approximately 143 Indigenous languages were lost, and Spanish became the predominant language.

One significant factor of the Spanish language becoming so predominant in the country was religion. Franciscan monks were the first to initiate a literacy process to convert the natives to Catholicism. However, the native languages were far from forgotten. To this day, around 4,000 náhuatl words are part of the everyday spoken Spanish in Mexico, which makes it a unique dialect.

In addition to the native languages, neighboring countries have profoundly influenced Mexican Spanish. You'll find three main dialects throughout the country. The southern dialect has a significant influence from the Maya and Quiché languages, while the central dialect is the one most Mexicans identify with. Meanwhile, the northern dialect is known for incorporating many English words due to its proximity to the United States. Do not be surprised if you come across English words used casually in Mexican Spanish. This is a result of the media's influence on Mexican culture for more than thirty years.

Now that you grasp the evolution of Mexican Spanish, let's explore one of the most vital elements of the language: the alphabet and its sounds.

The Alphabet (El Alfabeto)

The Spanish alphabet currently consists of 27 letters. It includes all 26 letters used in the English alphabet and a unique letter, 'ñ'. Let's take a look at the Spanish alphabet and its pronunciation below.

- **A (ah):** As the 'a' in 'f**a**rm'
- **B (beh):** As the 'be' in '**be**tter'
- **C (seh):** As the 'se' in '**se**t'
- **D (deh):** As the 'th' in '**th**ey'
- **E (eh):** As the 'e' in '**e**gg'
- **F (eh-feh):** As the 'effe' in '**effe**ct'
- **G (heh):** As the 'he' in '**he**nce'
- **H (ah-cheh):** As the 'a' in '**a**rt' and 'che' in '**che**que'. Together 'ah-cheh'
- **I (e):** As the 'i' in 'f**i**t'
- **J (ho-thah):** As the 'ho' in '**ho**tel' and 'tah' in 'chee**tah**'. Together 'ho-tah'
- **K (kah):** As the 'k' in '**k**ite'
- **L (eh-leh):** As the 'ele' in '**ele**phant'
- **M (eh-meh):** As the 'eme' in '**eme**sis'
- **N (eh-neh):** As the 'ene' in 'b**ene**dict'
- **Ñ (eh-nyeh):** As the 'eny' in 'K**eny**a'
- **O (oh):** As the 'o' in '**o**at'
- **P (peh):** As the 'pe' in '**pe**n'
- **Q (ku):** As the 'ku' in '**Ku**weit'

- **R (eh-rreh):** As the 'e' in '**e**gg' and 're' in '**re**y' but with the trilled 'r'. Together 'eh-rreh'

- **S (eh-seh):** As the 'esse' in '**esse**nce'

- **T (theh):** As the 'the' in '**the**rapy'

- **U (ooo):** As the 'u' in '**U**ber'

- **V (ooo-beh):** As the 'u' in '**U**ber' and 'be' in '**be**n'. Together 'ooo-beh'

- **W (doh-bleh ooo):** As the 'double' in '**double**t' and 'u' in '**u**ber'. Together 'Doh-bleh-ooo'

- **X (eh-kees):** As the 'e' in '**e**ight' and 'kis' in '**kis**s'. Together 'eh-kis'

- **Y (yeh):** As the 'ye' in '**ye**t'

- **Z (seh-tah):** As the 'se' in '**se**t' and 'tah' in 'chee**tah**'. Together 'seh-tah'

Now that you know the alphabet, let's review how it functions in words and speech.

The Vowels (Las Vocales)

The vowels in Spanish are the same as those in English. However, as you may already know, there is a slight pronunciation difference. ***Remember, In Spanish, all five vowels make just one sound, and they don't change. All of them are short sounds that stay the same.***

- **A (ah):** As the 'a' in 'f**a**rm'

- **E (eh):** As the 'e' in '**e**gg'

- **I (e):** As the 'i' in 'f**i**t'

- **O (oh):** As the 'o' in '**o**at'

- **U (ooo):** As the 'u' in '**U**ber'

The Consonants (Las Consonantes)

There are 22 consonants in Spanish. Let's take a closer look at each letter.

B (Beh): The Spanish 'B' functions similarly to the English 'B'. It has a strong 'B' sound when it appears as the first letter of a word or after the 'N' or 'M' letter. However, when it appears elsewhere in a word, it has a soft 'B' sound. The 'B' in Spanish is also known as B grande (big b), B larga (long b), B alta (tall b), and B de burro (b as in 'burro'). Next to the five vowels, it sounds as follows-

- Ba - bah
- Be - beh
- Bi - bee
- Bo - boh
- Bu - buu

C (seh): The Spanish 'C' has two different pronunciations, which depend on the vowel that comes after it. When the vowel 'E' or 'I' follows it, the letter 'C' sounds like the English 'S', as in 'Century' or 'Cigar'. On the other hand, when the vowel 'A', 'O', or 'U' follows it, the letter 'C' sounds like the English 'K', as in 'Company' or 'Comb'. Next to the five vowels, it sounds as follows-

- Ca - kah
- Ce - seh
- Ci - see
- Co - koh
- Cu - kuu

D (deh): The closest English equivalent to the Spanish 'D' is 'th', as in 'they'. It's generally a softer sound than the English D sound. Next to the five vowels, it sounds as follows-

- Da - thah
- De - theh
- Di - thee

- Do - thoh
- Du - thuu

F (eh-feh): The Spanish 'F' functions like the English 'F'. Next to the five vowels, it sounds as follows-

- Fa - fah
- Fe - feh
- Fi - fee
- Fo - foh
- Fu - fuu

G (heh): The Spanish 'G' has two different pronunciations, depending on the vowel that comes after it. If the letter 'G' is followed by 'E' or 'I', it sounds similar to the English 'H' but raspier. It is also known as a soft 'G'. On the other hand, if the letter 'G' is followed by 'A', 'O', or 'U', then it sounds similar to the English hard 'G'. Next to the five vowels, it sounds as follows-

- Ga - gah
- Ge - heh
- Gi - hee
- Go - goh
- Gu - guu

H (ah-Cheh): The Spanish 'H' is silent, except when it follows the letter 'C'. The 'C' and 'H' together make the 'CH' sound, as in chocolate. Next to the five vowels, it sounds as follows-

- Ha - ah
- He - eh
- Hi - ee
- Ho - oh

- Hu - uu

J (ho-tah): The Spanish 'J' is pronounced similarly to the English 'H' but is raspier, and the sound comes from the back of your throat. It sounds like the 'h' in 'hot'. Next to the five vowels, it sounds as follows-

- Ja - hah
- Je - heh
- Ji - hee
- Jo - hoh
- Ju - huu

K (kah): The Spanish 'K' functions like the English 'K'. Next to the five vowels, it sounds as follows-

- Ka - kah
- Ke - keh
- Ki - kee
- Ko - koh
- Ku - kuu

L (eh-leh): The Spanish 'L' functions like the English 'L'. Next to the five vowels, it sounds as follows-

- La - lah
- Le - leh
- Li - lee
- Lo - loh
- Lu - luu

M (eh-meh): The Spanish 'M' functions like the English 'M'. Next to the five vowels, it sounds as follows-

- Ma - mah
- Me - meh
- Mi - mee
- Mo - moh
- Mu - muu

N (eh-neh): The Spanish 'N' functions like the English 'N'. Next to the five vowels, it sounds as follows-

- Na - nah
- Ne - neh
- Ni - nee
- No - noh
- Nu - nuu

Ñ (eh-nyeh): This is a unique-sounding Spanish letter. Its pronunciation would be like the combinations of 'ni + vowel' as in words 'Califor**nia**' and 'o**nio**n', and 'ny + vowel' as in 'Ke**nya**' or 'ca**nyo**n'. Next to the five vowels, it sounds as follows-

- Ña - nyah
- Ñe - nyeh
- Ñi - nyee
- Ño - nyoh
- Ñu - nyuu

P (peh): The Spanish 'P' functions like the English 'P' but with less air. Next to the five vowels, it sounds as follows-

- Pa - pah
- Pe - peh
- Pi - pee
- Po - poh
- Pu - puu

Q (ku): The Spanish 'Q' functions like the English 'K'. Next to the five vowels, it sounds as follows-

- Qa - kah
- Qe - keh
- Qi - kee
- Qo - koh
- Qu - kuu

R (eh-rreh): The Spanish 'R' has two different pronunciations. The soft 'R', sounds similar to the English 'tt' in words like 'butter' or 'potter', and the strong 'R' is a rolled 'R' sound. I'll explain more about the rolled 'R' later. **Remember, the 'R' is rolled if it's at the beginning of a word or if you see 'double R (RR)' or after the letter L, N, or S.** Sometimes, it is also rolled at the end to add emphasis. Next to the five vowels, it sounds as follows-

- Ra - rrah
- Re - rreh
- Ri - rree
- Ro - rroh
- Ru - rruu

S (eh-seh): The Spanish 'S' functions like the English 'S'. Next to the five vowels, it sounds as follows-

- Sa - sah
- Se - seh
- Si - see
- So - soh
- Su - suu

T (theh): The Spanish 'T' is never aspirated when pronounced. It sounds more like a combination of 'T' and 'D'. To produce the 'T' sound in Spanish, place the tip of your tongue against the back of your top teeth to momentarily stop the airflow and then release it quickly. Next to the five vowels, it sounds as follows-

- Ta - tah
- Te - teh
- Ti - tee
- To - toh
- Tu - tuu

V (Ooo-veh): The Spanish 'V' functions similarly to the English 'B'. The 'V' in Spanish is also known as V chica (small v), V pequeña (small v), V corta (short v) and V de vaca (v as in 'cow'). Next to the five vowels, it sounds as follows-

- Va - bah
- Ve - beh
- Vi - bee
- Vo - boh
- Vu - buu

W (doh-bleh Ooo): The Spanish 'W' functions like the English 'W'. However, it is not a commonly used letter in Spanish and is usually found in words borrowed from English,

German, or languages like Chinese or Korean. When it comes to words borrowed from German, the letter 'W' is pronounced as 'b', such as in the word Wagner (pronounced as Bahg-nehr), which means the musician. For words borrowed from English, the letter 'W' is pronounced as 'U' in some cases, such as in the word Newton (pronounced as Nee-uu-tohn). For words borrowed from Chinese or Korean, the letter 'W' is pronounced as 'Gu', such as in the word Taiwán (pronounced as Tah-ee-gu-ahn), which means Taiwan. Next to the five vowels, it sounds as follows-

- Wa - wah
- We - weh
- Wi - wee
- Wo - woh
- Wu - wuu

X (eh-kees): The Spanish 'X' is pronounced like 'ks' or 'sh', similar to English. However, in words like México (Meh-hi-co) and Texas (Teh-has), it is pronounced like the Spanish 'J'. Next to the five vowels, it sounds as follows-

- Xa - xah
- Xe - xeh
- Xi - xee
- Xo - xoh
- Xu - xuu

Y (yeh): The Spanish 'Y' has two different pronunciations. When 'y' is on its own or appears at the end of a word, it is pronounced like the letter 'i' in Spanish. When 'y' is next to a vowel, it is pronounced similarly to 'LL' (doble ele). Its pronunciation can vary by region and may sound like the 'y' in 'yawn' or the 'j' in 'jam'. Next to the five vowels, it sounds as follows-

- Ya - yah/jah
- Ye - yeh/jeh

- Yi - yee/jee

- Yo - yoh/joh

- Yu - yuu/juu

Z (seh-tah): The Spanish 'Z' is pronounced like the English 'S'. Next to the five vowels, it sounds as follows-

- Za - sah

- Ze - seh

- Zi - see

- Zo - soh

- Zu - suu

Now, let's explore letter pairs that represent a single sound called digraphs.

CH: The 'CH' sound is the same as in the word 'chocolate', which I mentioned earlier with the letter 'H'.

RR: The 'RR' sound is the rolled 'R' sound. This sound takes practice (or you could be a natural) but is widely used in Spanish. It can be intimidating since it sounds so strong, but I suggest you start pronouncing the word 'throw' and slowly adding more 'rrr' to the word. Try to relax while doing it and keep practicing. That way, you'll get your tongue used to the movement and eventually pronounce it like a pro! Here's a short video that may help you to perfect it- https://www.youtube.com/shorts/gKwEuHdvgcM

GU: You will encounter this sound in the 'I' and 'E' combinations. The first combination, 'GUI', is pronounced 'gui' like in 'guitar', while the second, 'GUE', is pronounced 'geh', similar to 'ghetto'. You must skip the 'U' and pronounce the 'i' and 'e' directly. There is an exception to this rule. When two dots are on top of the letter 'u', called the 'umlaut', The 'ü' must be pronounced. For example, the word 'cigüeña' (stork). Without it, the word would be pronounced as 'cigeña'. Not many words use the umlaut, so keeping an eye on this element is essential.

QU: This is much like the 'GU' pair. You'll also encounter this sound in the 'I' and 'E' combinations. Like the above example of 'GU', you must skip the 'U' and pronounce the 'I' and 'E' directly. The first combination, 'QUE', is pronounced as 'keh' (like in 'ketchup'), and the second, 'QUI', is pronounced as 'ki' (like in 'kiosk').

LL: Lastly, there is the 'LL' sound, also known as 'doble ele'. Its pronunciation varies by region, sounding like 'y' in 'yawn' or 'j' in 'jam', as I mentioned earlier. It's worth noting that in some places like Argentina and regions of Uruguay, the 'LL' is pronounced more like 'sh' in English. For example, the word 'pollo' (meaning chicken) is pronounced as 'poh-sho'. Nevertheless, most Spanish-speaking countries follow the standard pronunciation guidelines covered above, so there's no need to worry about it. Just choose one pronunciation, stick to it, and move on.

Now that you know the alphabet and its sound, let's put them into practice. Please write your first and last name below and spell each letter out loud in Spanish.

- First name:
- Last name:

When you feel confident, record yourself speaking using your phone or any recording device, then listen back to ensure it is clear enough to understand.

Once you've mastered spelling your name, it's a good idea to practice spelling other important information relevant to you. Practicing these scenarios can enhance your communication skills and boost your confidence in real-life situations.

Syllables, Stress, and Accent Marks

Understanding syllables, stress, and accent marks is another essential aspect of achieving fluency in a language. This will enable you to read Spanish fluently.

Let's start with the syllables.

Syllables (Sílabas)

What are Syllables? Syllables are the fundamental units of sound that make up a word and are like building blocks that help you pronounce words correctly. For example-

- Cup (one syllable)
- Ta-ble (two syllables)
- Fan-tas-tic (three syllables)

There are two kinds of syllables in Spanish. The open, which ends in a vowel, and the closed, which ends in a consonant. For example-

Open syllables

- Ca-sa (house)
- Só-ta-no (basement)
- Ma-le-ta (Suitcase)

Closed syllables

- Cos-tar (to cost)
- Man-dar (to send)
- Char-lar (to chat)

Vowels are essential components of syllables. One of the important things you need to know about Spanish vowels is that they are categorized into two groups.

The strong vowels - A, E, O

The weak vowels - I, U

This is important because the pairing of vowels determines whether they belong to the same syllable or are separate.

Take a closer look at the rules below-

Rule no.1: Two strong vowels together make two different syllables. For example-

Caer (to fall): The letters 'a' and 'e' are strong vowels, so this will have two syllables, Ca-er.

Rule no.2: A consonant between two vowels makes a syllable with the second vowel. For example-

Casa (house): The consonant 's' lies between the two 'a' vowels, so the 's' will share a syllable with the second 'a', ca-sa.

Rule no.3: Two consonants together make two different syllables. For example-

Canto (sing): The letters 'n' and 't' are both consonants, so this will have two syllables, Can-to.

Exceptions: There is one exception to this rule, as there are some pairs of consonants that are unbreakable, and these are called 'Sílabas trabadas' in Spanish. These include pr, pl, br, bl, ll, rr, fr, fl, gr, gl, cr, cl, dr, tr, and tl.

For example-

Primo (male cousin): The letters 'p' and 'r' are together here, so they are unbreakable. They share the same syllable. You can also see the consonant 'm' between the vowels 'i' and 'o,' so rule no.2 applies here too. This means the consonant 'm' will share the same syllable with the second vowel 'o', Pri-mo.

Rule no.4: If three or more consonants appear between two vowels, the first consonants usually share the same syllable with the preceding vowel, while the next two consonants are grouped with the next vowel.

For example-

Empleados (Employees): The three consonants 'm', 'p', and 'l' are positioned between the two 'e' vowels. As a result, the first 'm' consonant will share the same syllable with the preceding 'e' vowel, while the following two consonants, 'p' and 'l,' will share the same syllable with the next 'e' vowel.

Additionally, the consonant 'd' is situated between the vowels 'a' and 'o'; thus, the second rule applies here as well. This means the consonant 'd' will share the same syllable with the second vowel 'o', Em-ple-a-dos.

Rule no.5: A strong vowel next to a weak vowel creates a diphthong, so they share the same syllable and blend their sounds.

For example-

Hielo (ice): The letter 'i' is a weak vowel, and 'e' is a strong vowel. Together, they create a diphthong and share the same syllable, H**ie**-lo.

Rule no.6: Two weak vowels together also share the same syllable.

For example-

Ciudad (city): The letters 'i' and 'u' are weak vowels, so they share the same syllable, C**iu**-dad.

Rule no.7: A strong vowel next to two weak vowels creates a triphthong, so they share the same syllable.

For example-

Buey (ox): In this word, the letter 'y' at the end is treated like the letter 'i.' Therefore, you have two weak vowels, 'u' and 'i,' and the strong vowel 'e,' which creates a triphthong. As a result, they share the same syllable, B**uey**.

Exceptions: When an accent is placed on a weak vowel, it transforms into a strong vowel. Once this change occurs, rule no.1 applies.

For example-

País (country): The letter 'a' is a strong vowel, and the letter 'i' is a weak vowel, but with the accent, it becomes a strong vowel, creating its own syllable, P**a**-**ís**.

Rule no.8: Last but not least, the prefixes have their own syllables.

For example-

Descubrir (to discover): The prefix 'des' is used in this word, so it will have a syllable of its own, Des-cu-brir.

Stress

Now, what about stress? Stress is a term articulated with emphasis on a syllable to express significance. For example-

- **TA**-ble (the stress is on the first syllable)

- fan-**TAS**-tic (the stress is on the second syllable)

- a-ca-**DE**-mic (the stress is on the third syllable)

There are three stress rules in Spanish that tell you where to stress. The stress rules are as follows-

Rule no.1: If a word ends in n, s, or a vowel, the stress is on the second-to-last syllable. For example-

- **ME**-sa (table) - the stress falls on the first syllable.

- a-**BRI**-go (coat) - the stress falls on the second syllable.

- pa-sa-**POR**-te (passport) - the stress falls on the third syllable.

Rule no.2: If rule number one does not apply, the stress is on the final syllable. For example-

- fe-**LIZ** (happy)

- es-pa-**ÑOL** (Spanish)

- es-tu-di-**AR** (study)

Rule no.3: If a word has an accent mark, the above rules do not apply. The accent indicates which syllable to stress, so stress where you see the accent mark. For example-

-pa-**PÁ** (dad)

-**CÁ**-ma-ra (camera)

-te-**LÉ**-fo-no (telephone)

Accent Marks

Now that you understand syllables and stress, let's discuss accent marks.

Accent marks are essential for effective communication, as their placement can alter the meaning of a word. For instance, 'si' without an accent means 'if,' while 'sí' with an accent means 'yes.' Therefore, checking the accent marks is essential to avoid confusion.

There are three accent marks in the Spanish language -

The acute accent (á) - The acute accent is only used with vowels to indicate the stressed syllable in a word. This will look like á, é, í, ó, and ú.

The tilde (ñ) - The tilde is a small wavy line above the letter 'n' that has 'ny' sounds like in Ca**ny**on.

The umlaut (ü) - The umlaut is a small two dots that appear on the letter 'u' to indicate that it should be pronounced. It produces a sound similar to the 'u' in 'r**u**de.' An example of a Spanish word with the letter 'u' with umlaut is 'pingüino', which means penguin in English.

You now understand what syllables, stress, and accent marks are and how they function in Spanish. Let's put this knowledge into practice.

Exercise 1

Identify the syllables and capitalize the stressed syllables for the following list of words.

For example:

recompensa - re-com-PEN-sa (Also, try pronouncing them out loud as you write the answer.)

    a) Amigo -

    b) Croar -

    c) Negativo -

    d) Mantequilla -

    e) Capa -

    f) Mago -

    g) Ducha -

    h) Doblado -

    i) Aspiradora -

    j) Cautiverio -

    k) Aventura -

    l) Multiplicar -

    m) Inundar -

    n) Comida -

    o) Sauna -

    p) Casa -

    q) Bebible -

    r) Castillo -

s) Manicomio -

t) Punta -

u) El Mañana -

v) Bengala -

w) Carga -

x) Sirena -

y) Original -

z) Música -

[Note: Answers are on pages 207-208.]

Nouns

Nouns in Spanish are words that identify a person, place, or thing. All nouns in Spanish have a gender: either masculine or feminine. Objects like books, bags, and houses have gender; however, this doesn't mean they are physically male or female. The gender of a noun in Spanish is just a grammatical feature. The only time a noun's gender in Spanish corresponds to a living being's actual gender is when explicitly referring to that living being.

The gender of a noun can often be identified by its ending; however, be aware that there are exceptions. The noun's gender also influences the forms of other associated words, such as articles, pronouns, and adjectives. Let's begin by discussing the gender of living nouns.

The Gender of Living Nouns

As I mentioned earlier, a noun's gender in Spanish only corresponds to the actual gender of a living being when it explicitly refers to that being. Therefore, if the being referred to is male, the noun will be masculine; if the being is female, the noun will be feminine. For example-

- hombre (man) [masculine]
- mujer (woman) [feminine]
- padre (father) [masculine]
- madre (mother) [feminine]

When Discussing Things in General

It is common for people to use the masculine form of living nouns by default when discussing things in general. This doesn't necessarily mean they assume the thing being discussed is male. If you would like to specify that the noun is female, one common way to do so is by replacing the 'o' ending with an 'a'. For example-

- chic**o** (boy) to chic**a** (girl)
- herman**o** (brother) to herman**a** (sister)

- gat**o** (cat) to gat**a** (female cat)

- perr**o** (dog) to perr**a** (female dog)

Like the above, in many professions and job titles, you can simply **add 'a' at the end** of the word to refer to a female. For example-

- profesor (teacher) to profesor**a** (female teacher)

- doctor (doctor) to doctor**a** (female doctor)

- pintor (painter) to pintor**a** (female painter)

When Discussing The Genders of a Group

Remember, *when discussing the genders of a group that includes both males and females, the group is always considered masculine, regardless of the number of males or females present.* For example, if there are five women and only one or two men, the group is still considered masculine and referred to as 'hombres.' However, *if there are only women, it is considered feminine* and referred to as 'mujeres.' This rule applies to other words, too, such as 'abuelos' for male and female grandparents and 'abuelas' for only grandmothers.

Animals that have Only One Gender

Some animals have only one gender. *To specify them as male or female, you need to add 'macho' (male) or 'hembra' (female) after the animal's name.* For example, 'canguro **macho**' (**male** kangaroo) or 'canguro **hembra**' (**female** kangaroo).

Here is a list of some animals that have one gender-

Masculine

- Chimpancé (Chimpanzee)

- Canguro (Kangaroo)

- Gorila (Gorilla)

- Rinoceronte (Rhinoceros)

- Murciélago (Bat)
- Pájaro (Bird)
- Mosquito (Mosquito)
- Pez (Fish)
- Delfín (Dolphin)
- Tiburón (Shark)

Feminine
- Ardilla (Squirrel)
- Cebra (Zebra)
- Jirafa (Giraffe)
- Rana (Frog)
- Ballena (Whale)
- Abeja (Bee)
- Cucaracha (Cockroach)
- Rata (Rat)
- Tortuga (Turtle)
- Ballena (Whale)

Word Endings that are Invariable

Some word endings are invariable. In this case, *only the article changes to reflect masculine and feminine gender.* For example-

- un turista/una turista (a tourist)
- un rehén/una rehén (a hostage)

- un testigo/una testigo (a witness)

In the example above, the article 'un' is used for masculine nouns and 'una' for feminine nouns, which is equivalent to the English article 'a.' You'll learn more about the articles later.

Now, let's move on to the gender of non-living nouns.

The Gender of Non-living Nouns

The gender of non-living nouns can be identified by the following rules; however, be aware of the exceptions as well.

Rules for Masculine Nouns

Rule no.1: Nouns that end in 'o' are usually masculine, for example, teléfon**o** (telephone), muse**o** (museum), and diner**o** (money).

Exceptions: Some words ending in 'o' in Spanish are feminine because they are abbreviated and retain the original gender. For instance, 'moto' is the abbreviation of 'motocicleta (motorcycle)' and is, therefore, feminine. Likewise, 'foto' is the abbreviation of 'fotografía (photography)' and is feminine. Some other words that end in 'o' but are feminine are- mano (hand), radio (radio), etc.

Rule no.2: Nouns ending in 'l' are usually masculine, for example, pape**l** (paper) and materia**l** (material).

Exceptions: Some feminine words ending in 'l' include cárcel (prison), sal (salt), miel (honey), etc.

Rule no.3: Nouns ending in 'n' and 'ion' are usually masculine. For example, nouns ending in 'n' include jabó**n** (soap), botó**n** (button), and colchó**n** (mattress), and nouns ending in 'ión' include cam**ión** (truck), av**ión** (airplane), and bast**ión** (stronghold).

Exceptions: Some feminine words ending in 'n' and 'ión' include sartén (frying pan), imagen (image), razón (reason), nación (nation), reunión (meeting), opinión (opinion), confusión (confusion), religión (religion), canción (song), etc.

Rule no.4: Nouns ending in 'r' are usually masculine, for example, colo**r** (color), favo**r** (favor), moto**r** (motor), etc.

Exceptions: Some feminine words ending in 'r' include labor (labor) and flor (flower).

Rule no.5: Nouns ending in 's' are typically masculine. This rule only applies to nouns that **naturally have an 's' at the end** in their singular form, for example, análisi**s** (analysis), interé**s** (interest), and me**s** (month).

Exceptions: Some feminine words ending in 's', 'sis', and 'itis' include res (beef), mies (harvest), tos (cough), diabetes (diabetes), dosis (dose), crisis (crisis), tesis (thesis), bronquitis (bronchitis), apendicitis (appendicitis), artritis (arthritis), etc.

Rule no.6: Nouns ending in an 'accented vowel' are usually masculine, for example, t**é** (tea), caf**é** (coffee), and tis**ú** (tissue).

Rule no.7: Nouns ending in 'aje' and 'ambre' are usually masculine, for example, equip**aje** (luggage), vi**aje** (trip), and cal**ambre** (cramp).

Exceptions: Some feminine words that are exceptions to this are hambre (hunger) and pelambre (thick hair).

Rule no.8: Nouns ending in 'e' could be masculine or feminine. One way to identify its gender is by examining the article before it. Some masculine nouns that end in 'e' are - el perfum**e** (the perfume), el coch**e** (the car), and el restaurant**e** (the restaurant).

Exceptions: Some feminine nouns that end in 'e' are- la frase (the phrase), la calle (the street), la clase (the class), etc.

In the above examples, **the article 'el' is the masculine form of 'the'** for masculine nouns, and **'la' is the feminine form of 'the'** for feminine nouns.

Now, let's move on to the rules for feminine nouns.

Rules for Feminine Nouns

Rule no.1: Nouns that end in 'a' are usually feminine, for example, cas**a** (house), camis**a** (shirt), and carter**a** (wallet).

Exceptions: ***Some words ending in 'a' are masculine due to their Greek origin or other foreign language roots.*** *They usually have* ***'ma', 'pa', and 'ta' endings****, for example, proble**ma** (problem), ma**pa** (map), plane**ta** (planet), etc.*

Rule no.2: Nouns ending in 'd' are usually feminine, for example, felicida**d** (happiness), ciuda**d** (city), and verda**d** (truth).

Exceptions: Some masculine words ending in 'd' include césped (grass), ardid (scheme), and ataúd (coffin).

Rule no.3: Nouns ending in 'z' are usually feminine, for example, vo**z** (voice), lu**z** (light), and pa**z** (peace).

Exceptions: Some masculine words ending in 'z' include haz (bundle), lápiz (pencil), arroz (rice), pez (fish), matiz (shade), etc.

Rule no.4: Nouns ending in 'ie', 'nte', and 'umbre' are usually feminine, for example, superfic**ie** (surface), fue**nte** (fountain), and c**umbre** (summit).

Exceptions: Some masculine words that are exceptions to this are puente (bridge), diente (tooth), etc.

I completely understand that there's a lot to take in! So **don't stress about trying to memorize it all at once.** A great place to start is to remember that nouns ending in **'o' are usually masculine**, while those ending in **'a' are typically feminine.** This will help you get it right most of the time. You've got this!

Nouns that can be Both Genders

Some nouns can be both genders and have two meanings. Here is a list of some nouns that have multiple meanings depending on the context:

Masculine	Feminine

El mañana (tomorrow/the future)	La mañana (morning)
El papa (pope)	La papa (potato)
El capital (capital as in finance)	La capital (capital as in a city)
El parte (message/report)	La parte (part/portion)
El cólera (cholera)	La cólera (anger)
El coma (coma)	La coma (comma)
El cometa (comet)	La cometa (kite)
El corte (cut)	La corte (Court)
El cura (priest)	La cura (cure)
El pendiente (earring)	La pendiente (Slope)

Plural Nouns

A plural noun is a noun that signifies more than one person, place, thing, or concept. For example, 'cat' in its plural form will be 'cats,' just as 'dog' in its plural form will be 'dogs.'

Here are some guidelines to help you correctly form plural nouns in Spanish.

Pluralizing Nouns

Add '-s'

- ❖ If the noun ends in a vowel. For example-
    - manzana (apple) to manzana**s** (apples)
    - camisa (shirt) to camisa**s** (shirts)

    Note: Nouns that end with stressed í or ú vowels can have two plural forms: you can either add 's' or 'es' at the end. Both options are correct.

- ❖ If the noun ends in a consonant other than n, r, s, l, j, d, or y. For example-
    - iceberg (iceberg) to iceberg**s** (icebergs)
    - zigzag (zigzag) to zigzag**s** (zigzags)

Add '-es'

- ❖ If the noun ends in a consonant n, r, s, l, j, d, or y. For example-
    - camión (bus) to camion**es** (buses)
    - sartén (frying pan) to sartén**es** (frying pans)

    Note: When a word is borrowed from another language and ends with 'y,' the plural form is created by dropping the 'y' and adding 'is.'

    Additionally, some nouns that end with 's' may retain the same form in both singular and plural. This typically happens to singular nouns with two or more syllables ending in a vowel (without an accent) followed by 's.' In such cases, only the article needs to be changed. For example,

- **El** paraguas (The umbrella) to **Los** paraguas (The umbrellas)
- **La** tesis (The thesis) to **Las** tesis (The theses)

In the example above, ***the article 'Los' is the masculine plural form of 'the'*** for masculine nouns, whereas ***'Las' is the feminine plural form of 'the'*** for feminine nouns.

Add '-ces'

- ❖ If the noun ends in 'z'. When a noun ends with the letter 'z' in Spanish, it follows a rule that is similar to rules in English. In English, when a word ends in 'f', such as 'loaf' or 'calf', the plural is formed by replacing the 'f' with 'v' and adding 'es'. For example, 'loaf' becomes 'loa**ves**', and 'calf' becomes 'cal**ves**'. In the same way, when a noun in Spanish ends in 'z', it changes to 'c' and then adds 'es' to form the plural. For example-
    - lápi**z** (pencil) to Lápi**ces** (pencils)
    - raí**z** (root) to Raí**ces** (roots)

Uncountable Nouns

Additionally, certain nouns in Spanish are classified as uncountable. These nouns refer to substances, concepts, or abstract ideas. For example-

- Agua (Water)
- Aire (air)

These are not usually used in plural form or preceded by a specific number. ***If you use these nouns in plural form, it means you are referring to different types or units of the same matter.***

Articles (A, an & the)

As you explored nouns and plural nouns, you encountered some articles through some examples. You may already know what 'a' and 'the' are in Spanish or maybe not. Anyway, let's explore this topic further in this chapter to gain a clearer understanding.

Nouns are usually accompanied by articles such as 'a,' 'an,' or 'the.' These articles fall into two categories: definite and indefinite. You use the definite article 'the' when referring to something specific and the indefinite article 'a' or 'an' when discussing something in general.

In Spanish, the forms of articles are determined by the noun's gender. This means that how you say 'the' and 'a/an' in Spanish will vary depending on whether the noun is masculine or feminine and whether it is singular or plural. To understand better, look at the following tables that outline the different forms of articles in Spanish.

Definite Article	The	
	Masculine	*Feminine*
Singular	el	la
Plural	los	las

Indefinite Article	A/an	
	Masculine	*Feminine*

Singular	un	una
Plural	unos	unas

Here are some examples-

Definite Article	**The**	
	Masculine	*Feminine*
Singular	El libro (The book)	La casa (The house)
Plural	Los libros (The books)	Las casas (The houses)

Indefinite Article	**A/an**	
	Masculine	*Feminine*
Singular	Un libro (A book)	Una casa (A house)
Plural	Unos libros (Some books)	Unas casas (Some houses)

Note: When dealing with feminine nouns that begin with a stressed 'a' or 'ha,' it's important to remember that they take the masculine article in the singular form. This rule is primarily based on phonetic reasons; having two 'a' sounds would make it difficult to differentiate between the first syllable of the noun and the last part of the article. For example, the noun 'arte' uses the masculine article 'el,' resulting in 'el arte,' even though 'arte' is a feminine noun. However, when the noun becomes plural, it takes the feminine article 'las,' resulting in 'las artes.' The 's' in 'las' helps eliminate phonetic ambiguity, allowing for smoother pronunciation.

Now that you have a good understanding of Spanish nouns and articles, let's put this knowledge into practice.

Exercise 2

Identify the gender of the following nouns. Write 'f' if it is feminine and 'm' if it is masculine.

a) yegua -

b) teléfono -

c) mañana -

d) música -

e) nieve -

f) escritorio -

g) árbol -

h) guitarra -

i) fiesta -

j) piedra -

k) violin -

l) nube -

m) fotografía -

n) mano -

o) pie -

p) reloj -

q) mueble -

r) computadora -

Now add the Spanish article 'el' or 'la' before the nouns depending on their genders.

a) ___ yegua

b) ___ teléfono

c) ___ mañana

d) ___ música

e) ___ nieve

f) ___ escritorio

g) ___ árbol

h) ___ guitarra

i) ___ fiesta

j) ___ piedra

k) ___ violin

l) ___ nube

m) ___ fotografía

n) ___ mano

o) ___ pie

p) ___ reloj

q) ___ mueble

r) ___ computadora

Exercise 2.1

Write the following words in plural forms.

a) el candado -

b) el animal -

c) el gato -

d) el árbol -

e) la llave -

f) la casa -

g) el espejo -

h) la tienda -

i) la canción -

[Note: Answers are on pages 208-209.]

Numbers

Clear communication often requires using numbers to express quantities, time, date, distance, and other concepts. Whether buying groceries or telling time, mastering numbers can significantly help you around and improve your communication and language skills. It may take some practice and time to become comfortable with these Spanish numbers; however, the more you practice, the easier it will become.

One of the differences in Spanish numbers is that **you use a period to separate big numbers and commas for numbers less than 1**, which is contrary to how you use them in English. For example - 1,000,000 will be 1.000.000, and 0.5 will be 0,5 in Spanish.

Now, without further ado, let's explore the world of Spanish numbers.

Cardinal Numbers

Cardinal numbers are just the basic counting numbers used to determine the quantity of items. Let's start from 0 to 20:

0 - cero

1 - uno

2 - dos

3 - tres

4 - cuatro

5 - cinco

6 - seis

7 - siete

8 - ocho

9 - nueve

10 - diez

11 - once

12 - doce

13 - trece

14 - catorce

15 - quince

16 - dieciséis

17 - diecisiete

18 - dieciocho

19 - diecinueve

20 - veinte

For numbers 21 to 29, the format will be slightly different.

21 - veintiuno

22 - veintidós

23 - veintitrés

24 - veinticuatro

25 - veinticinco

26 - veintiséis

27 - veintisiete

28 - veintiocho

29 - veintinueve

Once you reach 29, counting up to 100 in Spanish becomes easier. Just follow this simple formula outlined below-

Formula: Root number + y (and) + Numbers from 1 to 9

For example-

- Treinta (thirty) + y (and) + uno (one) = Treinta y uno, which is 'thirty-one' in Spanish.
- Cuarenta (forty) + y (and) + dos (two) = Cuarenta y dos, which is 'forty-two' in Spanish.

And so on…

Here are the root numbers you need to count from 30-100.

30 - Treinta

40 - Cuarenta

50 - Cincuenta

60 - Sesenta

70 - Setenta

80 - Ochenta

90 - Noventa

100 - Cien / Ciento

Remember, when you add a number to 100, 'cien' changes to 'ciento.' Once you know 1-100, you can learn to count the rest of the numbers easily, as they follow a similar pattern.

Formula: Root number + Numbers from 1 to 99

For example-

- *Ciento (100) + treinta (30) = Ciento treinta, which is 'one hundred and thirty'.*
- *Doscientos (200) + treinta (30) + y (and) + uno (one) = Doscientos treinta y uno, which is 'two hundred and thirty-one'.*

You may notice another difference between English and Spanish when using the conjunction 'and' when expressing numbers. In English, the word 'and' is used after the hundreds, such as in 'one hundred and twenty-three.' However, in Spanish, this conjunction does not come after the hundreds. **The only time you use 'and' in Spanish is between a tens place and one's place to indicate that these two numbers combine to form one number.**

For example-

- *'Cincuenta y tres', which translates to 50 and 3, forming 53.*
- *'Doscientos cincuenta y tres', which literally translates to 200,50 and 3, forming 253.*

Here are the root numbers to count from 200-999.

200 - Doscientos

300 - Trescientos

400 - Cuatrocientos

500 - Quinientos

600 - Seiscientos

700 - Setecientos

800 - Ochocientos

900 - Novecientos

When discussing the numbers from 200 to 900 in Spanish, it's important to remember that these figures are expressed in their plural forms, ending with an 's', as they represent multiples of 100. For instance, 'ciento' transforms into 'cientos'.

Additionally, remember that when these numbers are used with nouns, they will take on masculine or feminine forms depending on the gender of the noun they modify. For example, consider the number 500: when referring to '500 books,' you would say 'quinientos libros,' using the masculine form. In contrast, when speaking about '500 magazines,' you would use the feminine form, saying 'quinientas revistas.'

Now that you know how to count the numbers from 0 to 999. You need two root numbers to count up to a million.

- 1.000 (mil)
- 1.000.000 (un millón)

Counting from mil to un millón is pretty straightforward and similar to English. Just follow this simple formula outlined below-

Formula: <u>Any number + mil (thousand) or millón (million)</u>.

For example-

- *Dos (two) + mil (thousand) = Dos mil, which is 'two thousand' in Spanish.*
- *Treinta (three) y (and) cinco (five) + mil (thousand) = Treinta y cinco mil, which is 'thirty-five thousand' in Spanish.*
- *Tres (Three) + millón (million) = Tres millón, which is 'three million' in Spanish.*
- *Treinta (three) y (and) cinco (five) + millón (million) = Treinta y cinco millón, which is 'thirty-five million' in Spanish.*

When counting a number that is 'thousand' or 'million' **<u>something</u>**, such as 'two thousand **<u>three hundred and ten</u>**' or 'two million **<u>three hundred and ten</u>**', you simply place that number after 'mil' (thousand) or 'millón' (million).

For example-

- *Dos (two) + mil (thousand) + trescientos diez (three hundred and ten) = **<u>Dos mil trescientos diez</u>**, which is '**<u>two thousand three hundred and ten</u>**' in Spanish.*
- *Dos (two) + millón (million) + trescientos diez (three hundred and ten) = **<u>Dos millón trescientos diez</u>**, which is '**<u>two million three hundred and ten</u>**' in Spanish.*

I hope you get the idea.

One common mistake an English speaker may make is to use 'un' with 'mil' when referring to 'a thousand' or 'one thousand.' While it's understandable why some might make this error, it's important to avoid saying 'un mil.' The correct usage is simply 'mil' when referring to one thousand. *The only time 'un mil' should be used is for numbers like-*

- 31.000 (treinta y un mil), which translates to **thirty and one thousand**, which is 31.000 (thirty-one thousand).

- 41.000 (cuarenta y un mil), which translates to **forty and one thousand**, which is 41.000 (forty-one thousand).

And so on...

Note: 'Mil' remains the same in plural form.

From one million, you might anticipate it to be one billion next, as in English; however, this is where things change significantly in Spanish. The Spanish equivalent to one billion is 'mil millones/millardo (1.000.000.000).' After that, you'll have 'un billón (1.000.000.000.000),' which is equivalent to one trillion. Then 'mil billones (1.000.000.000.000.000)' equivalent to one quadrillion. Lastly, 'un trillón (1.000.000.000.000.000.000),' which is equivalent to one quintillion. Take a look at the table below to see the differences more clearly:

English	Spanish
1,000,000 (One Million)	1.000.000 (Un Millón)
1,000,000,000 (One Billion)	1.000.000.000 (Mil Millones/Millardo)
1,000,000,000,000 (One Trillion)	1.000.000.000.000 (Un Billón)
1,000,000,000,000,000 (One Quadrillion)	1.000.000.000.000.000 (Mil Billones)
1,000,000,000,000,000,000 (One Quintillion)	1.000.000.000.000.000.000 (Un Trillón)

Saying '...and a half' in Spanish

In English, condensing numbers using phrases like '…and a half' is common. So, instead of stating 'one thousand five hundred,' an English speaker might say 'one and a half thousand.' Instead of 'one million five hundred thousand,' they might say 'one and a half million.'

In Spanish, 'and a half' is translated as 'y medio'. How you implement this phrase with numbers like the above differs slightly in Spanish. For instance, **'one and a half thousand' is written as 'one thousand and a half' (Mil y medio)**, and **'one and a half million' as 'one million and a half' (Un millón y medio).** This pattern can be applied to other numbers as well.

For example-

- *One and a half (Uno y medio)*
- *Two and a half (Dos y medio)*
- *One hundred and a half (Cien y medio)*

Now, it's time to learn about Ordinal Numbers.

Ordinal Numbers

Ordinal numbers indicate the position or order of an object or person in a sequence, such as '1st' (first), '2nd' (second), and '3rd' (third). They correspond in gender and number to the nouns they describe. The ordinal numbers from 1 to 10 are:

First - Primero

Second - Segundo

Third - Tercero

Fourth - Cuarto

Fifth - Quinto

Sixth - Sexto

Seventh - Séptimo

Eighth - Octavo

Ninth - Noveno

Tenth - Décimo

To form ordinal numbers from 10, you need to know the root numbers similar to the cardinal number. Below is the formula-

Formula: Root number + Ordinal numbers from 1 to 9

For example-

- *Vigésimo primero (Twenty first)*
- *Trigésimo segundo (Thirty second)*

Here are the root numbers.

Twentieth - Vigésimo

Thirtieth - Trigésimo

Fortieth - Cuadragésimo

Fiftieth - Quincuagésimo

Sixtieth - Sexagésimo

Seventieth - Septuagésimo

Eightieth - Octogésimo

Ninetieth - Nonagésimo

Hundredth - Centésimo

Note: For the numbers ranging from '11th' to '19th,' write them in one word, for instance, 'decimosegundo (twelfth)', decimotercero (thirteenth), decimocuarto (fourteenth), etc.

Now that you understand cardinal and ordinal numbers in Spanish, let's put this knowledge into practice.

Exercise 3

Write the following cardinal numbers in Spanish.

a) 32 -

b) 56 -

c) 94 -

d) 195 -

e) 396 -

f) 798 -

g) 1.132 -

h) 4.341 -

i) 9.832 -

j) 10.341 -

k) 51.556 -

l) 72.761 -

m) 112.445 -

n) 556.789 -

o) 890.987 -

p) 1.000.000 -

q) 1.000.000.000 -

r) 1.000.000.000.000 -

Exercise 3.1

Write the following ordinal numbers in Spanish.

a) 12th -

b) 25th -

c) 34th -

d) 49th -

e) 55th -

f) 67th -

g) 78th -

h) 84th -

i) 99th -

[Note: Answers are on pages 209-210.]

Time

Learning to ask and express time in Spanish is essential as it helps you navigate your surroundings more effectively. To ask about the current time, you can simply use one of the following phrases:

- ¿Que hora es? (What time is it? [The standard way.])

- ¿Que horas son? (What time is it? [Use this phrase when you're sure it isn't one o'clock. As you can see, the phrase is plural. It's a more casual way to ask time.])

- ¿Me das la hora? (Can you give me the time?)

- ¿Me dices la hora? (Can you tell me the time?)

- ¿Que hora tienes? (What time do you have? [This phrase is used to inquire about the time on someone's watch, clock, cellphone, etc.])

To respond, say 'Es la una' when it's one o'clock or use 'Son las' followed by the appropriate hour for any other time. For example-

- Son las dos. (It's two o'clock.)

- Son las tres. (It's three o'clock.)

- Son las cuatro. (It's four o'clock.)

Let's look at the diagram below to help you understand the time if it is not precisely on the hour.

In the diagram, you'll see the first half of the clock on the right-hand side using 'y' (meaning 'and') followed by whatever the minute is to the hour and the other half of the clock on the left-hand side using 'menos' (meaning 'minus') followed by whatever the minute is to the hour. The 'menos' minutes are the reverse of the 'y' minutes. The basic formula for telling the time that is precisely not on the hour is-

Formula: Es la/Son las + hour + y/menos + minute

Let's examine the time from 4 to 5 o'clock for an example.

- *Son las cuatro en punto. (It's four o'clock.)*
- *Son las cuatro y cinco. (It's five past four.)*
- *Son las cuatro y diez. (It's ten past four.)*
- *Son las cuatro y cuarto. (It's a quarter past four.)*
- *Son las cuatro y veinte. (It's twenty past four.)*
- *Son las cuatro y veinticinco. (It's twenty-five past four.)*
- *Son las cuatro y media. (It's half past four.)*
- *Son las cinco menos veinticinco. (It's twenty-five to five.)*
- *Son las cinco menos veinte. (It's twenty-to-five.)*
- *Son las cinco menos cuarto. (It's a quarter to five.)*
- *Son las cinco menos diez. (It's ten to five.)*
- *Son las cinco menos cinco. (It's five to five.)*
- *Son las cinco en punto. (It's five o'clock.)*

Another common way to tell time in Mexico is to omit the words 'y' and 'menos' except for the 15- and 30-minute marks. Unlike the earlier method, when the time is past the half-hour mark, you simply add the number of minutes instead of subtracting them.

For example-

- *Son las cuatro en punto. (It's four o'clock.)*
- *Son las cuatro cinco. (It's four o-five.)*
- *Son las cuatro diez. (It's four ten.)*
- *Son las cuatro y cuarto or Son las cuatro quince. (It's a quarter past four, or It's four fifteen.)*
- *Son las cuatro veinte. (It's four twenty.)*
- *Son las cuatro veinticinco. (It's four twenty-five.)*
- *Son las cuatro y media or Son las cuatro treinta. (It's half past four, or it's four thirty)*
- *Son las cuatro treinta y cinco (It's four thirty-five.)*
- *Son las cuatro cuarenta (It's four forty.)*
- *Son las cuatro cuarenta y cinco (It's four forty-five.)*
- *Son las cuatro cincuenta (It's four fifty.)*
- *Son las cuatro cincuenta y cinco (It's four fifty-five.)*
- *Son las cinco en punto. (It's five o'clock.)*

There are also a few other alternative ways to tell the time for the second half of the hour, such as using the words 'para' and 'faltan' to convey a similar meaning as 'menos'. In this context, 'para' means 'to' or 'until,' while 'faltan' means 'it's lacking', which is the conjugated form of the verb 'faltar,' which means 'to lack' or 'to be left.' Take a look at the following examples.

Example 1

- *Son veinticinco **para** las cinco. (It's twenty-five **to/until** five)*
- *Son veinte **para** las cinco. (It's twenty **to/until** five)*
- *Son quince **para** las cinco. (It's fifteen **to/until** five.)*
- *Son diez **para** las cinco. (It's ten **to/until** five.)*

- *Son cinco **para** las cinco. (It's five **to/until** five.)*

Example 2

- ***Faltan** veinticinco **para** las cinco. (**It's lacking** twenty-five **to/until** five)*
- ***Faltan** veinte **para** las cinco. (**It's lacking** twenty **to/until** five)*
- ***Faltan** quince **para** las cinco. (**It's lacking** fifteen **to/until** five.)*
- ***Faltan** diez **para** las cinco. (**It's lacking** ten **to/until** five.)*
- ***Faltan** cinco **para** las cinco. (**It's lacking** five **to/until** five.)*

If you want to specify the time of the day, add one of the following phrases at the end.

- De la mañana (in the morning) - From sunrise to noon.
- De la tarde (in the afternoon/evening) - From noon to sunset.
- De la noche (in the evening/night) - After sunset to sunrise.

Note: 'De' translates to 'of,' and 'la' translates to 'the' in English. However, in this context, they are understood as 'in the' or 'at' when specifying the time of day. This is because the Spanish language functions differently, so translations do not always correspond directly.

For example-

- *Son las siete **de la mañana**. (It's seven **in the morning.**)*
- *Son las ocho menos cinco **de la mañana.** (It's five to eight **in the morning.**)*
- *Es la una **de la tarde.** (It's one **in the afternoon.**)*
- *Son las dos y cinco **de la tarde.** (It's five past two **in the afternoon.**)*
- *Son las ocho **de la noche.** (It's eight **at night.**)*
- *Son las nueve menos cinco **de la noche.** (It's five to nine **at night.**)*

Time-Related Vocabulary

- Hora- hour/time
- Horas - hours/times
- Minuto - Minute
- Minutos - Minutes
- Segundo - Second
- Segundos - Seconds
- Un cuarto para - A quarter to
- Media - Half
- Día - Day
- Hoy - Today
- Mediodía - Midday/noon
- Medianoche - Midnight

Days, Months & Dates

Now that you've got everything you need to express time, let's dive into days, months, and dates.

Days

- domingo - Sunday
- lunes - Monday
- martes - Tuesday
- miércoles - Wednesday

- jueves - Thursday
- viernes - Friday
- sábado - Saturday

Note: The days of the week are not capitalized in Spanish.

Here are some common ways to express days-

- ❖ **A simple way to express 'Today is _____' would be:**

    → Hoy es **(whatever the day is today)**.

    For example-

    - *Hoy es **domingo**. (Today is **Sunday**.)*

- ❖ **To express 'Tomorrow is _____' would be:**

    → Mañana es **(whatever the day is tomorrow)**.

    For example-

    - *Mañana es **lunes**. (Tomorrow is **Monday**.)*

- ❖ **To express 'The day after tomorrow is _____' would be:**

    → Pasado mañana es **(whatever the day after tomorrow is)**.

    For example-

    - *Pasado mañana es **martes**. (The day after tomorrow is **Tuesday**.)*

- ❖ **To express 'Yesterday was _____' would be:**

    → Ayer fue **(whatever the day was yesterday)**.

    For example-

    - *Ayer fue **sábado**. (Yesterday was **Saturday**.)*

❖ **To express '*The day before yesterday was _____*' would be:**

→ Anteayer fue **(whatever the day before yesterday was)**.

For example-

- *Anteayer fue **viernes**. (The day before yesterday was **Friday**.)*

Months

- enero - January
- febrero - February
- marzo - March
- abril - April
- mayo - May
- junio - June
- julio - July
- agosto - August
- septiembre - September
- octubre - October
- noviembre - November
- diciembre - December

Note: The months are also not capitalized in Spanish.

Dates

In Spanish, dates are formatted similarly to the UK, following the day/month/year (DD/MM/YYYY) structure. They can be separated by periods, dashes, or slashes, and there's no need for a leading zero with single-digit days or months. It is also common to omit the first two digits of the year.

To inquire about today's date, you could say:

- *¿Cuál es la fecha de hoy? (What is today's date?)*

To respond to that, you could say:

→ Hoy es el **(whatever the Day is)** de **(whatever the month is)** de **(whatever the year is)**.

For example-

- *Hoy es el **dos** de **marzo** de **dos mil veinticuatro**. (Today is the **2nd** of **march 2024**)*

In Spanish, dates are expressed using cardinal numbers, except for the first day of the month, which uses ordinal numbers.

For example-

- *Hoy es el **primero** de marzo de dos mil veinticuatro. (Today is the **1st** of march 2024)*

Now that you understand how to express time, days, months, and dates in Spanish, let's put this knowledge into practice.

Answer the following questions in Spanish depending on the current day you're in, and practice speaking them out loud by yourself or with your friend, taking turns to ask or answer them in Spanish-

- ¿Qué día es hoy? (What day is today?)

    -

- ¿Qué hora es? (What time is it?)

    -

- ¿Qué fecha es hoy? (What date is today?)

-

- ¿Qué día es mañana? (What day is tomorrow?)

  -

- ¿Qué día es pasado mañana? (What day is the day after tomorrow?)

  -

- ¿Qué día fue ayer? (What day was yesterday?)

  -

- ¿Qué día fue anteayer? (What day was the day before yesterday?)

  -

How to say I, You, He, She, etc

In this chapter, you'll explore the basic subject pronouns in Spanish, such as 'I,' 'you,' 'he,' 'she,' etc. These pronouns are essential because they help you avoid repeating the same noun over and over, making your sentences flow better.

Also, please note that 'vosotros' is not commonly used in Mexico, so it will not be covered here. Take some time to familiarize yourself with these pronouns, as they are essential for conjugating verbs later.

Subject Pronouns:

- Yo - I
- Tú - You (informal)
- Usted - You (formal)
- Ustedes - You all (formal and informal)
- Él - He
- Ella - She
- Nosotros (masculine) / Nosotras (feminine) - We
- Ellos (masculine) / Ellas (feminine) - They

Adjectives

Adjectives are very handy words that give us details about something or someone, as well as info about time and places. They must agree with the nouns they describe in Spanish regarding gender and number.

In Spanish, most adjectives come after the nouns they describe. This includes adjectives related to size, color, shape, and personality. Some writers may occasionally mix up the order for stylistic reasons. However, I recommend you adhere to the standard arrangement.

There are also some certain adjectives that come before the noun. For instance, Adjectives of quantity or number usually come before the noun. So, just be mindful of these exceptions.

Let's go over the types of adjectives now.

Descriptive Adjectives

A descriptive adjective gives additional information about the noun it refers to, including details about its look, feel, or other attributes. They usually **come after the noun** they modify. Here are some common descriptive adjectives-

English	Masculine	Feminine	Plural
Happy	Feliz	Feliz	Felices
Sad	Triste	Triste	Tristes
Good	Bueno	Buena	Buenos/ Buenas
Bad	Mal	Mala	Malos/Malas

Pretty	Bonito	Bonita	Bonitos/Bonitas
Ugly	Feo	Fea	Feos/Feas
Great	Gran	Gran	Grandes
Big	Grande	Grande	Grandes
Small	Pequeño	Pequeña	Pequeños/Pequeñas
Tall	Alto	Alta	Altos/Altas
Short	Bajo	Baja	Bajos/Bajas
Quick	Rápido	Rápida	Rápidos/Rápidas
Slow	Lento	Lenta	Lentos/Lentas
Warm	Caliente	Caliente	Calientes
Cold	Frío	Fría	Fríos/Frías
Expensive	Caro	Cara	Caros/Caras

Cheap	Barato	Barata	Baratos/ Baratas
Simple	Sencillo	Sencilla	Sencillos/ Sencillas
Complicated	Complicado	Complicada	Complicados/ Complicadas
Fun	Divertido	Divertida	Divertidos/ Divertidas
Boring	Aburrido	Aburrida	Aburridos/ Aburridas
Interesting	Interesante	Interesante	Interesantes
Beautiful	Hermoso	Hermosa	Hermosos/ Hermosas
Known	Conocido	Conocida	Conocidos/ Conocidas
Unknown	Desconocido	Desconocida	Desconocidos/ Desconocidas

Strange	Extraño	Extraña	Extraños/Extrañas
Familiar	Familiar	Familiar	Familiares
Local	Local	Local	Locales
Foreign	Extranjero	Extranjera	Extranjeros/Extranjeras
Public	Público	Pública	Públicos/Públicas
Private	Privado	Privada	Privados/Privadas
Lazy	Flojo	Floja	Flojos/Flojas
Hardworking	Trabajador	Trabajadora	Trabajadores/Trabajadoras
Kind	Amable	Amable	Amables
Rude	Grosero	Grosera	Groseros/Groseras
Strong	Fuerte	Fuerte	Fuertes

Weak	Débil	Débil	Débiles
Thin	Delgado	Delgada	Delgados/ Delgadas
Fat	Gordo	Gorda	Gordos/ Gordas
Smart/ intelligent	Inteligente	Inteligente	Inteligentes
Dumb	Tonto	Tonta	Tontos/Tontas

For example-

- *La casa **grande**. (The **big** house.)*
- *El carro **azul**. (The **blue** car.)*
- *El hombre **fuerte**. (The **strong** man.)*
- *El clima **frío**. (The **cold** weather.)*

Demonstrative Adjectives (This, that, these, and those)

A demonstrative adjective is a word used to point out or indicate a particular noun in a sentence. They **come right before the noun** they describe.

Singular

English	Masculine	Feminine	Distance
this	este	esta	close
that	ese	esa	near
that	aquel	aquella	far

Plural

English	Masculine	Feminine	Distance
these	estos	estas	close
those	esos	esas	near
those	aquellos	aquellas	far

For example-

Singular

- ***Este*** *libro. (**This** book.)*
- ***Ese*** *libro. (**That** book. [Near to you])*
- ***Aquel*** *libro. (**That** book over there. [Far from you])*

Plural

- ***Estos*** *libros. (**These** books.)*
- ***Esos*** *libros. (**Those** books. [Near to you])*

- ***Aquellos** libros. (**Those** books over there. [Far from you])*

Note: You also have 'esto,' meaning 'this,' and 'eso,' meaning 'that.' Both are genderless and are used when you don't know what something is or as a pronoun when referring to a situation, phenomenon, or thing that hasn't been mentioned before.

For example-

- *Qué es **esto**? (What is **this**?)*
- *¡**Esto** es bueno! (**This** is good!)*
- *Qué es **eso**? (What is **that**?)*
- *¡**Eso** es terrible! (**That** is terrible!)*

Possessive Adjectives

Possessive adjectives provide details about the ownership of a noun, indicating who or what the noun belongs to.

There are two forms of possessive adjectives: short and long form. They serve the same purpose, but the long form emphasizes ownership more. **The short form comes before,** and **the long form comes after the noun** it modifies.

Short form

English	Masculine	Feminine	Plural
my	mi	mi	mis
your (informal)	tu	tu	tus
his/her/its/ your (formal)	su	su	sus

our	nuestro	nuestra	nuestros/ nuestras
their/your (plural)	su	su	sus

For example-

- *¿Has visto **mi** teléfono? (Have you seen **my** phone?)*
- *Me encanta **tu** camiseta. (I love **your** t-shirt.)*
- *¿Te dio **su** dirección? (Did he give you **his** address?)*
- *Él es **nuestro** amigo. (He is **our** friend.)*

Long-form

English	Masculine	Feminine	Plural
mine	mío	mía	míos/mías
yours	tuyo	tuya	tuyos/tuyas
his/hers/its/ yours (formal)	suyo	suya	suyos/suyas
ours	nuestro	nuestra	nuestros/ nuestras
theirs/yours (plural)	suyo	suya	suyos/suyas

For example-

- *¿Viste a un amigo **nuestro**? (Did you see a friend of **ours**?)*
- *Conocí a unos colegas **suyos**. (I met some of **his** colleagues.)*
- *Ellos son amigos **míos**. (They are friends of **mine**.)*
- *Me gustan esas pinturas **tuyas**. (I like those paintings of **yours**.)*

It's important to remember that these long-form possessive adjectives in Spanish **can also act as possessive pronouns**, which can cause some confusion. The key difference is that **possessive adjectives describe nouns**, while **possessive pronouns fully replace them**.

For example-

Possessive adjective: *__Mi__ carro es azul. (__My__ car is blue.)*

Possessive pronoun: *El carro azul es __mío__. (The blue car is __mine__.)*

Numeric Adjectives

Numeric adjectives are adjectives used to describe nouns' quantity or order. They include cardinal numbers (one, two, three, etc.) and ordinal numbers (first, second, third, etc). They **usually come before the noun**.

For example-

- *Tengo __dos__ hermanos. (I have __two__ brothers.)*
- *Mi __segundo__ libro. (My __second__ book.)*

Numerical adjectives in Spanish have some exceptions and special rules. For instance, **'uno' changes to 'un'** when it precedes a masculine noun, as in 'un libro' (a book), and 'una' when it precedes a feminine noun, as in 'una casa' (a house). Numbers ending in uno, like Veintiuno (Twenty-one) or Treinta y uno (Thirty-one), also undergo these changes.

Ordinal numbers primero and tercero also lose the final '-o' when they are before a singular noun. This happens regardless of whether another word precedes the noun.

*For example, Mi **primer** viaje gratis. (My **first** free ride.)*

Indefinite Adjectives

Indefinite adjectives serve as a general method to express the quantity of specific nouns in a non-specific manner. They **_usually come before the noun_**.

English	Masculine	Feminine	Plural
A/an/some/any	algún	alguna	algunos/algunas
Many/a lot of/much	mucho	mucha	muchos/muchas
Little/few	poco	poca	pocos/pocas
Several	n/a	n/a	varios/varias
Certain	cierto	cierta	ciertos/ciertas
Any	cualquier	cualquier	cualesquiera
Both	ambos	ambas	n/a
All/everybody	todo	toda	todos/todas
Not a single/no/any	ningún	ninguna	ningunos/ningunas

Enough	bastante	bastante	bastantes
Another/ Other	otro	otra	otros/otras
Each	cada	cada	n/a

For example-

- *Hay **poca** comida. (There's **little** food.)*

- *No tenemos **ningún** problema. (We don't have **any** problem.)*

- *Vamos a **otro** restaurante esta vez. (Let's go to **another** restaurant this time.)*

Relational Adjectives

Relational adjectives allow you to establish a connection between two nouns. Often, the nouns being connected are not explicitly mentioned, so these adjectives help you imply a relationship without stating it explicitly. These can be nationalities, places of origin, etc. They **usually come after the noun**.

Nationalities	Masculine	Feminine	Plural
African	africano	africana	africanos/ africanas
German	alemán	alemana	alemanes/ alemanas
Argentine	argentino	argentina	argentinos/

			argentinas
Brazilian	brasileño	brasileña	brasileños/ brasileñas
British	británico	británica	británicos/ británicas
Bolivian	boliviano	boliviana	bolivianos/ bolivianas
Canadian	canadiense	canadiense	canadienses
Chilean	chileno	chilena	chilenos/ chilenas
Chinese	chino	china	chinos/ chinas
Colombian	colombiano	colombiana	colombianos/ colombianas
Costa Rican	costarricense	costarricense	costarricenses
Cuban	cubano	cubana	cubanos/ cubanas
Danish	danés	danesa	daneses/

			danesas
Korean	coreano	coreana	coreanos/ coreanas
Dominican	dominicano	dominicana	dominicanos/ dominicanas
Ecuadoran	ecuatoriano	ecuatoriana	ecuatorianos/ ecuatorianas
Spanish	español	española	españoles/ españolas
French	francés	francesa	franceses/ francesas
Finnish	finlandés	finlandesa	finlandeses/ finlandesas
Guatemalan	guatemalteco	guatemalteca	guatemaltecos/ guatemaltecas
Honduran	hondureño	hondureña	hondureños/ hondureñas
Iraqi	iraquí	iraquí	iraquíes

Indian	indio	india	indios/ indias
English	inglés	inglesa	ingleses/ inglesas
Irish	irlandés	irlandesa	irlandeses/ irlandesas
Italian	italiano	italiana	italianos/ italianas
Japanese	japonés	japonesa	japoneses/ japonesas
Lebanese	libanés	libanesa	libaneses/ libanesas
Mexican	mexicano	mexicana	mexicanos/ mexicanas
Moroccan	marroquí	marroquí	marroquíes
Nepalese	nepalés	nepalesa	nepaleses/ nepalesas

Nicaraguan	nicaragüense	nicaragüense	nicaragüenses
Nigerian	nigeriano	nigeriana	nigerianos/ nigerianas
American	americano	americana	americanos/ americanas
Puerto Rican	puertorriqueño	puertorriqueña	puertorriqueños/ puertorriqueñas
Russian	ruso	rusa	rusos/rusas
Thai	tailandés	tailandesa	tailandeses/ tailandesas
Uruguayan	uruguayo	uruguaya	uruguayos/ uruguayas

For example-

- *Soy **mexicano**. (I'm **Mexican**.)*
- *Soy **africano**. (I'm **African**.)*
- *Soy **americano**. (I'm **American**.)*
- *Soy **británico**. (I'm **British**.)*

Note: Nationalities are not capitalized in Spanish unless they begin a sentence.

Prepositions

Prepositions are invariable and serve as connectors between different parts of a sentence, as well as introducing complements. Depending on the context, it can have various meanings, so knowing how to identify them is crucial in Spanish. The following list will help you learn the 22 main prepositions that Spanish has:

Preposition	English	Example
A	To, at	¿A dónde ir? (Where to go?)
Ante	Before, compared to	Ante la adversidad (Before the adversity)
Bajo	Under, below	Bajo la cama (Under the bed)
Con	With	Con mi familia (With my family)
Contra	Against	Contra el otro equipo (Against another team)
De	Of, from, about	De la escuela (Of the school)
Desde	From, since	Desde pequeño (Since little)
Durante	During, for	Durante mi vida (During my life)
En	In, into, at, on, by	En el mar (In the sea)
Entre	Between, among	Entre las calles (Between the streets)

Hacia	Towards, around	Hacia el futuro	(Towards the future)
Hasta	Until, as far as, up to	Hasta mañana	(Until tomorrow)
Mediante	Through, by means of	Mediante los datos	(Through the data)
Para	For, by, to, towards	Para ella	(For her)
Por	For, by, to, because of, through, per	Por ahora	(For now)
Salvo	Except	Salvo tú	(Except you)
Según	According to, depending on	Según tus gustos	(According to your taste)
Sin	Without	Sin miedo	(Without fear)
Sobre	On, on top of, over, above, upon, about	Sobre la caja	(On top of the box)
Tras	Behind, after	Tras la casa	(Behind the house)
Versus	Versus, against	México versus USA	(Mexico vs. USA)
Vía	By, via	Vía satélite	(Via satellite)

These prepositions can be divided into five different groups.

Place

- De - from (Use 'De' to indicate origin/source)
- Desde - from (Use 'Desde' to indicate the starting point)
- A - to (Use 'a' to indicate destination)
- Hacia - toward
- Hasta - until
- Sobre - on (Use 'Sobre' to indicate something is on top of or over an object)
- En - in/at/on (Use 'En' to indicate something is within another object)
- Ante - before
- Bajo - under/below
- Tras - behind
- Entre - between

Time

- Durante - during, for (Use 'Durante' as 'for' to indicate the duration of time)
- En - in (Use 'en' with days, months, and years)
- Tras - after
- De - from
- A - to/at
- Hasta - until
- Desde - since
- Entre - between

- Sobre - about
- Hacia - around

Cause

- De - of
- Por - for (Use 'por' to indicate the reason/cause behind something or when it benefits someone indirectly.)

Purpose

- A - to
- Para - for (Use 'para' to indicate a sort of aim, destination, recipient, or when it benefits someone directly.)

Manner

- Con - with
- Sin - without
- De - of
- En - in
- A - to
- Entre - among
- Contra - against
- Según - according to
- Vía - by/through

Common Prepositional Phrases Related to Place/Location

- Detrás de - behind
- Delante de - in front of (To indicate that something is at a closer distance)
- Enfrente de - in front of (To indicate that something is across from or faces a certain distance apart)
- Encima de - on top of
- Debajo de - under
- En medio de - in the middle of
- Cerca de - close to
- Lejos de - far from
- Alrededor de - around

The Fusion of Prepositions and Definite Articles

When 'de' or 'a' is followed by the definite article 'el', they combine to form 'del' or 'al'.

- de + el: del (of/from the)
- a + el: al (to/at the)

Exercise 4

Pronouns

1) What is the subject pronoun for 'You' (Informal)?

    a) Él

    b) Ella

    c) Yo

    d) Tú

2) What is the subject pronoun for 'You all'?

    a) Yo

    b) Tú

    c) Usted

    d) Ustedes

3) What is the subject pronoun for 'She'?

    a) Yo

    b) Él

    c) Ella

    d) Tú

4) What is the subject pronoun for 'We' (all women)?

    a) Él

    b) Ella

    c) Nosotros

    d) Nosotras

5) What is the subject pronoun for 'They' (all women)?

    a) Ellos

    b) Ellas

    c) Nosotros

    d) Nosotras

Exercise 4.1

Adjectives

1) What is the function of the adjective?

    a) Modify or describe nouns and pronouns

    b) Replace the nouns

    c) Connect nouns or pronouns to other words

    d) Express action or states of being

2) In Spanish, where do adjectives of size, shape, color, and personality usually go in a sentence?

    a) Before the noun

    b) After the noun

    c) After the verb

    d) Anywhere

3) In Spanish, where do adjectives of quantity or number usually go in a sentence?

    a) After the noun

    b) Before the noun

    c) Middle of the sentence

d) None of the above

4) What is the masculine form for 'this' in Spanish?

    a) Ese

    b) Esa

    c) Este

    d) Esta

5) What is the feminine form for 'those' when referring to objects or people near you?

    a) Este

    b) Esta

    c) Esos

    d) Esas

6) What is the masculine form for 'those' when referring to objects or people far from you?

    a) Esos

    b) Esas

    c) Aquellos

    d) Aquellas

7) What is the masculine form for 'mine' in Spanish?

    a) Tuyo

    b) Tuya

    c) Mío

    d) Mía

Exercise 4.2

Prepositions

The following sentences are missing their prepositions in Spanish. Choose the correct preposition for each sentence.

1) Escondió el vestido _____ el closet. (She hid the dress _____ the closet.)

    a) bajo

    b) en

    c) vía

    d) Ante

2) Lo enviaré _____ correo postal. (I will send it _____ postal mail.)

    a) por

    b) de

    c) para

    d) En

3) Este regalo lo compré _____ ti. (I bought this gift _____ you.)

    a) sobre

    b) para

    c) durante

    d) tras

4) Se resfrió _____ culpa del frío. (He caught a cold _____ of the cold.)

    a) por

    b) hasta

c) mediante

d) con

5) Escuché música _____ el viaje. (I listened to music _____ the trip.)

   a) sobre

   b) de

   c) durante

   d) versus

[Note: Answers are on pages 211-212.]

Verbs

Verbs are a fundamental part of any language. They tell you what the subject of the sentence is doing or, in some cases, what is happening to the subject. Understanding how Spanish verbs work is key to forming sentences, expressing ideas, and communicating effectively.

A verb in its base form is called **'The Infinitive'** and is equivalent to 'to [verb]' in English. For example, habl**ar** (to speak), com**er** (to eat), Viv**ir** (to live), etc. ***They all end in -ar, -er, or -ir in Spanish. These infinitives act as the root, from which all other conjugated verb forms are created.***

Conjugation

Like in many languages, Spanish verbs change their form depending on who is doing the action (the subject) and when the action is happening (the tense). These changes are called conjugations. In Spanish, ***conjugation involves changing the infinitive verb ending (-ar, -er, or -ir) depending on the subject and tense.***

There are three main tenses in Spanish: Presente (present), Pasado / Pretérito (past), and Futuro (future), and three moods/modes in which these tenses can be conjugated:

1. ***Indicativo (Indicative)***

    It expresses assertion, facts, and objective statements.

2. ***Subjunctive (Subjunctive)***

    It expresses reactions, feelings, doubts, or insecurities.

3. ***Imperativo (Imperative)***

    It gives direct orders and commands.

As a beginner, you'll be focusing on mastering the conjugation of the three basic tenses: simple present, past, and future, which you'll go through soon. Understanding these tenses will help you grasp the structures and patterns of verb conjugation in Spanish. This will make it easier for you to learn the rest.

In Spanish, as in English, there are two types of verbs: Regular and Irregular. Let's begin with the regular verbs.

Regular Verbs

Regular verbs are verbs that have a consistent pattern in their conjugation. This means that when you change their tense, they typically add a standard ending, such as '-ed', for the past tense in English.

For example-

- *'walk' becomes 'walked'*
- *'play' becomes 'played'*

And so on…

Let's now go over how they are conjugated in Spanish below.

Simple Present Tense Conjugation

This conjugation is used when discussing things happening at the moment, regularly, or as general truths. To conjugate a verb, you remove the -ar, -er, or -ir ending and add a new ending that tells you who is doing the action and when they did it. The ending for each type of verb goes as follows with the following subject pronouns:

Subject Pronouns	-ar verbs	-er verbs	-ir verbs
Yo (I)	-o	-o	-o
Tú (You [informal])	-as	-es	-es
Usted/Él/Ella (You [formal]/He/She/It)	-a	-e	-e

Nosotros [masculine]/Nosotras [feminine] (We)	-amos	-emos	-imos
Ustedes/Ellos/Ellas (You all/They)	-an	-en	-en

For example-

-ar: *Hablar (to speak)*

To conjugate this verb, you remove the '-ar' ending, which will result in Habl__, and add a new ending that tells you who is doing the action and when they did it with the help of the above table. For instance-

- I speak - Yo habl**o**
- You speak - Tú habl**as**
- You (Formal)/He/She/It speaks - Usted/Él/Ella habl**a**
- We speak - Nosotros/Nosotras habl**amos**
- You all/They speak - Ustedes/Ellos/Ellas habl**an**

-er: *Comer (to eat)*

To conjugate this verb, you remove the '-er' ending, which will result in Com__, and add a new ending that tells you who is doing the action and when they did it with the help of the earlier table. For instance-

- I eat - Yo com**o**
- You eat - Tú com**es**
- You (Formal)/He/She/It eats - Usted/Él/Ella com**e**
- We eat - Nosotros/Nosotras com**emos**

- You all/They eat - Ustedes/Ellos/Ellas com**en**

-ir: *Vivir (to live)*

To conjugate this verb, you remove the '-ir' ending, which will result in Viv__, and add a new ending that tells you who is doing the action and when they did it with the help of the earlier table. For instance-

- I live - Yo viv**o**
- You live - Tú viv**es**
- You (Formal)/He/She/It lives - Usted/Él/Ella viv**e**
- We live - Nosotros/Nosotras viv**imos**
- You all/They live - Ustedes/Ellos/Ellas viv**en**

Simple Past Tense Conjugation

This conjugation is used when talking about things and events that happened at a specific moment in the past. The ending for each type of verb goes as follows with the following subject pronouns:

Subject Pronouns	-ar verbs	-er verbs	-ir verbs
Yo (I)	-é	-í	-í
Tú (You [informal])	-aste	-iste	-iste
Usted/Él/Ella (You [formal]/He/She/It)	-ó	-ió	-ió

Nosotros [masculine]/Nosotras [feminine] (We)	-amos	-imos	-imos
Ustedes/Ellos/Ellas (You all/They)	-aron	-ieron	-ieron

Note: -er and -ir verbs have the same ending in the past tense.

For example-

-ar: Hablar (to speak)

To conjugate this verb, you remove the '-ar' ending, which will result in Habl__, and add a new ending that tells you who did the action and when they did it with the help of the above table. For instance-

- I spoke - Yo habl**é**
- You spoke - Tú habl**aste**
- You (Formal)/He/She/It spoke - Usted/Él/Ella habl**ó**
- We spoke - Nosotros/Nosotras habl**amos**
- You all/They spoke - Ustedes/Ellos/Ellas habl**aron**

-er: Comer (to eat)

To conjugate this verb, you remove the '-er' ending, which will result in Com__, and add a new ending that tells you who did the action and when they did it with the help of the earlier table. For instance-

- I ate - Yo com**í**
- You ate - Tú com**iste**
- You (Formal)/He/She/It ate - Usted/Él/Ella com**ió**

- We ate - Nosotros/Nosotras com**imos**
- You all/They ate - Ustedes/Ellos/Ellas com**ieron**

-ir: *Vivir (to live)*

To conjugate this verb, you remove the '-ir' ending, which will result in Viv__, and add a new ending that tells you who did the action and when they did it with the help of the earlier table. For instance-

- I lived - Yo viv**í**
- You lived - Tú viv**iste**
- You (Formal)/He/She/It lived - Usted/Él/Ella viv**ió**
- We lived - Nosotros/Nosotras viv**imos**
- You all/They lived - Ustedes/Ellos/Ellas viv**ieron**

Simple Future Tense Conjugation

This conjugation is used when discussing things and events that will happen at a specific moment. This is the easiest one of the three as the ending for each type of verb is the same, and you **don't need to remove the -ar, -er, and -ir endings** of the verb; *however, you need to add a new ending* that tells you who will do the action and when they will do it. The ending for each type of verb goes as follows with the following subject pronouns:

Subject Pronouns	-ar verbs	-er verbs	-ir verbs
Yo (I)	-é	-é	-é
Tú (You [informal])	-ás	-ás	-ás

Usted/Él/Ella (You [formal]/He/She/It)	-á	-á	-á
Nosotros [masculine]/Nosotras [feminine] (We)	-emos	-emos	-emos
Ustedes/Ellos/Ellas (You all/They)	-án	-án	-án

For example-

-ar: *Hablar (to speak)*

To conjugate this verb, add a new ending with the help of the above table. For instance-

- I will speak - Yo hablar**é**
- You will speak - Tú hablar**ás**
- You (Formal)/He/She/It will speak - Usted/Él/Ella hablar**á**
- We will speak - Nosotros/Nosotras hablar**emos**
- You all/They will speak - Ustedes/Ellos/Ellas hablar**án**

-er: *Comer (to eat)*

To conjugate this verb, add a new ending with the help of the earlier table. For instance-

- I will eat - Yo comer**é**
- You will eat - Tú comer**ás**
- You (Formal)/He/She/It will eat - Usted/Él/Ella comer**á**
- We will eat - Nosotros/Nosotras comer**emos**

- You all/They will eat - Ustedes/Ellos/Ellas comer**án**

-ir: *Vivir (to live)*

To conjugate this verb, add a new ending with the help of the earlier table. For instance-

- I will live - Yo vivir**é**
- You will live - Tú vivir**ás**
- You (Formal)/He/She/It will live - Usted/Él/Ella vivir**á**
- We will live - Nosotros/Nosotras vivir**emos**
- You all/They will live - Ustedes/Ellos/Ellas vivir**án**

Now, let's move onto the irregular verbs.

Irregular Verbs

Unlike regular verbs, irregular verbs do not have a consistent pattern in their conjugation. Because of their unique forms, these verbs often require memorization to be used correctly in different tenses.

For example-

- 'go' becomes 'went'
- 'be' becomes 'was/were'

And so on…

Let's go over some common and useful irregular verbs in Spanish below.

Ser and Estar (to be)

In Spanish, the verb 'to be' can be 'Ser' and 'Estar'.

Ser: Ser describes ***a permanent*** state or quality that is not expected to change over time, such as ***identity, origin, personal traits***, etc. The conjugation of 'Ser' goes as follows:

Subject Pronouns	Present Tense	Past Tense	Future Tense
Yo (I)	Soy (I am)	Fui (I was)	Seré (I will be)
Tú (You [informal])	Eres (You are)	Fuiste (You were)	Serás (You will be)
Usted/Él/Ella (You [formal]/He/She/It)	Es (You are or He/She/It is)	Fue (You were or He/She was)	Será (You/He/She will be)
Nosotros [masculine]/Nosotras [feminine] (We)	Somos (We are)	Fuimos (We were)	Seremos (We will be)
Ustedes/Ellos/Ellas (You all/They)	Son (You all/They are)	Fueron (You all/They were)	Serán (You all/They will be)

Estar: Estar describes *a temporary* state expected to change over time, such as *emotion, condition, action*, etc. The conjugation of 'Estar' goes as follows:

Subject Pronouns	Present Tense	Past Tense	Future Tense
Yo (I)	Estoy (I am)	Estuve (I was)	Estaré (I will be)
Tú (You [informal])	Estás (You are)	Estuviste (You were)	Estarás (You will be)
Usted/Él/Ella (You [formal]/He/She/It)	Está (You are or He/She/It is)	Estuvo (You were or He/She was)	Estará (You/He/She will be)

Nosotros [masculine]/Nosotras [feminine] (We)	Estamos (We are)	Estuvimos (We were)	Estaremos (We will be)
Ustedes/Ellos/Ellas (You all/They)	Están (You all/They are)	Estuvieron (You all/They were)	Estarán (You all/They will be)

They can be confusing at the beginning, so the two acronyms below may help you remember the general uses of 'ser' and 'estar.' For 'ser,' remember 'DOCTOR,' and 'estar,' remember 'PLACE.'

Ser:

- Description - David **es** alto. (David **is** tall.)
- Occupation - **Él es** médico. (**He is** a doctor.)
- Characteristic - **Él es** inteligente. (**He is** smart.)
- Time - Hoy **es** jueves. (Today **is** Thursday.)
- Origin - **Somos** de México. (**We are** from Mexico.)
- Relations - **Él es** mi hermano. (**He is** my brother.)

Estar:

- Position - **Estoy** sentado. (**I'm** sitting.)
- Location - **Estoy** en la tienda. (**I'm** at the shop.)
- Action - **Estoy** comiendo. (**I'm** eating.)
- Condition - **Está** enfermo. (**He is** sick.)
- Emotion - **Estoy** feliz. (**I'm** happy.)

Ir (to go)

The verb 'Ir' means 'to go'. The conjugation of 'Ir' goes as follows:

Subject Pronouns	Present Tense	Past Tense	Future Tense
Yo (I)	Voy (I go)	Fui (I went)	Iré (I will go)
Tú (You [informal])	Vas (You go)	Fuiste (You went)	Irás (You will go)
Usted/Él/Ella (You [formal]/He/She/It)	Va (You go or He/She/It goes)	Fue (You/He/She went)	Irá (You/He/She will go)
Nosotros [masculine]/Nosotras [feminine] (We)	Vamos (We go)	Fuimos (We went)	Iremos (We will go)
Ustedes/Ellos/Ellas (You all/They)	Van (You all/They go)	Fueron (You all/They went)	Irán (You all/They will go)

Note: The past tense of this verb is identical to the past tense of 'Ser (to be).' You can determine which conjugated verb form this is by examining the context.

Venir (to come)

The verb 'Venir' means 'to come'. The conjugation of 'Venir' goes as follows:

Subject Pronouns	Present Tense	Past Tense	Future Tense
Yo (I)	Vengo (I come)	Vine (I came)	Vendré (I will come)

Tú (You [informal])	Vienes (You come)	Viniste (You came)	Vendrás (You will come)
Usted/Él/Ella (You [formal]/He/She/It)	Viene (You come or He/She/It comes)	Vino (You/He/She came)	Vendrá (You/He/She will come)
Nosotros [masculine]/Nosotras [feminine] (We)	Venimos (We come)	Vinimos (We came)	Vendremos (We will come)
Ustedes/Ellos/Ellas (You all/They)	Vienen (You all/They come)	Vinieron (You all/They came)	Vendrán (You all/They will come)

Decir (to say)

The verb 'Decir' means 'to say'. The conjugation of 'Decir' goes as follows:

Subject Pronouns	Present Tense	Past Tense	Future Tense
Yo (I)	Digo (I say)	Dije (I said)	Diré (I will say)
Tú (You [informal])	Dices (You say)	Dijiste (You said)	Dirás (You will say)
Usted/Él/Ella (You [formal]/He/She/It)	Dice (You say or He/She/It says)	Dijo (You/He/She said)	Dirá (You/He/She will say)
Nosotros [masculine]/Nosotras [feminine] (We)	Decimos (We say)	Dijimos (We said)	Diremos (We will say)

| Ustedes/Ellos/Ellas (You all/They) | Dicen (You all/They say) | Dijeron (You all/They said) | Dirán (You all/They will say) |

Dar (to give)

The verb 'Dar' means 'to give'. The conjugation of 'Dar' goes as follows:

Subject Pronouns	Present Tense	Past Tense	Future Tense
Yo (I)	Doy (I give)	Di (I gave)	Daré (I will give)
Tú (You [informal])	Das (You give)	Diste (You gave)	Darás (You will give)
Usted/Él/Ella (You [formal]/He/She/It)	Da (You give or He/She/It gives)	Dio (You/He/She gave)	Dará (You/He/She will give)
Nosotros [masculine]/Nosotras [feminine] (We)	Damos (We give)	Dimos (We gave)	Daremos (We will give)
Ustedes/Ellos/Ellas (You all/They)	Dan (You all/They give)	Dieron (You all/They gave)	Darán (You all/They will give)

Ver (to see)

The verb 'Ver' means 'to see'. The conjugation of 'Ver' goes as follows:

Subject Pronouns	Present Tense	Past Tense	Future Tense

Yo (I)	Veo (I see)	Vi (I saw)	Veré (I will see)
Tú (You [informal])	Ves (You see)	Viste (You saw)	Verás (You will see)
Usted/Él/Ella (You [formal]/He/She/It)	Ve (You see, or He/She/It sees)	Vió (You/He/She/It saw)	Verá (You/He/She/It will see)
Nosotros [masculine]/Nosotras [feminine] (We)	Vemos (We see)	Vimos (We saw)	Veremos (We will see)
Ustedes/Ellos/Ellas (You all/They)	Ven (You all/They see)	Vieron (You all/They saw)	Verán (You all/They will see)

Tener (to have)

The verb 'Tener' means 'to have'. The conjugation of 'Tener' goes as follows:

Subject Pronouns	Present Tense	Past Tense	Future Tense
Yo (I)	Tengo (I have)	Tuve (I had)	Tendré (I will have)
Tú (You [informal])	Tienes (You have)	Tuviste (You had)	Tendrás (You will have)
Usted/Él/Ella (You [formal]/He/She/It)	Tiene (You have or He/She has)	Tuvo (You/He/She had)	Tendrá (You/He/She will have)

Nosotros [masculine]/Nosotras [feminine] (We)	Tenemos (We have)	Tuvimos (We had)	Tendremos (We will have)
Ustedes/Ellos/Ellas (You all/They)	Tienen (You all/They have)	Tuvieron (You all/They had)	Tendrán (You all/They will have)

In addition to denoting possession, the verb 'tener' is utilized in various idiomatic expressions. For instance:

- Tener sed (to be thirsty)
- Tener hambre (to be hungry)
- Tener frío/calor (to be cold/hot)

The verb 'tener' is also frequently combined with other verbs to convey different actions and states:

- Tener que (to have to)
- Tener ganas de (to feel like / To want to.)

Hacer (to do)

The verb 'Hacer' means 'to do,' but it can also mean 'to make,' depending on the context. The conjugation of 'Hacer' goes as follows:

Subject Pronouns	**Present Tense**	**Past Tense**	**Future Tense**
Yo (I)	Hago (I do)	Hice (I did)	Haré (I will do)
Tú (You [informal])	Haces (You do)	Hiciste (You did)	Harás (You will do)

Usted/Él/Ella (You [formal]/He/She/It)	Hace (You do or He/She does)	Hizo (You/He/She did)	Hará (You/He/She will do)
Nosotros [masculine]/Nosotras [feminine] (We)	Hacemos (We do)	Hizimos (We did)	Haremos (We will do)
Ustedes/Ellos/Ellas (You all/They)	Hacen (You all/They do)	Hicieron (You all/They did)	Harán (You all/They will do)

Podar (to be able to)

The verb 'Podar' means 'can' or 'able to.' The conjugation of 'Podar' goes as follows:

Subject Pronouns	Present Tense	Past Tense	Future Tense
Yo (I)	Puedo (I can)	Pude (I was able to)	Podré (I will be able to)
Tú (You [informal])	Puedes (You can)	Pudiste (You were able to)	Podrás (You will be able to)
Usted/Él/Ella (You [formal]/He/She/It)	Puede (You/He/She can)	Pudo (You/He/She were able to)	Podrá (You/He/She will be able to)
Nosotros [masculine]/Nosotras [feminine] (We)	Podemos (We can)	Pudimos (We were able to)	Podremos (We will be able to)

| Ustedes/Ellos/Ellas (You all/They) | Pueden (You all/They can) | Pudieron (You all/They were able to) | Podrán (You all/They will be able to) |

Saber (to know)

The verb 'Saber' means 'to know,' referring to information such as facts or knowing how to do something. The conjugation of 'Saber' goes as follows:

Subject Pronouns	Present Tense	Past Tense	Future Tense
Yo (I)	Sé (I know)	Supe (I knew)	Sabré (I will know)
Tú (You [informal])	Sabes (You know)	Supiste (You knew)	Sabrás (You will know)
Usted/Él/Ella (You [formal]/He/She/It)	Sabe (You know or He/She knows)	Supo (You/He/She knew)	Sabrá (You/He/She will know)
Nosotros [masculine]/Nosotras [feminine] (We)	Sabemos (We know)	Supimos (We knew)	Sabremos (We will know)
Ustedes/Ellos/Ellas (You all/They)	Saben (You all/They know)	Supieron (You all/They knew)	Sabrán (You all/They will know)

Querer (to want)

The verb 'Querer' can mean 'to want' when referring to objects and 'to love' when referring to people in a more casual sense, such as between friends, starting a new relationship, or showing appreciation for someone in your life. The conjugation of 'Querer' goes as follows:

Subject Pronouns	Present Tense	Past Tense	Future Tense
Yo (I)	Quiero (I want)	Quise (I wanted)	Querré (I will want)
Tú (You [informal])	Quieres (You want)	Quisiste (You wanted)	Querrás (You will want)
Usted/Él/Ella (You [formal]/He/She/It)	Quiere (You want or He/She wants)	Quiso (You/He/She wanted)	Querrá (You/He/She will want)
Nosotros [masculine]/Nosotras [feminine] (We)	Queremos (We want)	Quisimos (We wanted)	Querremos (We will want)
Ustedes/Ellos/Ellas (You all/They)	Quieren (You all/They want)	Quisieron (You all/They wanted)	Querrán (You all/They will want)

Poner (to put)

The verb 'Poner' generally means 'to put' or 'to place.' It is commonly used to describe the action of placing something in a specific location or position. However, it can have various other meanings and is often used in different idiomatic expressions, so its translations can vary depending on the context. The conjugation of 'Poner' goes as follows:

Subject Pronouns	Present Tense	Past Tense	Future Tense
Yo (I)	Pongo (I put)	Puse (I put)	Pondré (I will put)
Tú (You [informal])	Pones (You put)	Pusiste (You put)	Pondrás (You will put)

Usted/Él/Ella (You [formal]/He/She/It)	Pone (You put or He/She puts)	Puso (You/He/She put)	Pondrá (You/He/She will put)
Nosotros [masculine]/Nosotras [feminine] (We)	Ponemos (We put)	Pusimos (We put)	Pondremos (We will put)
Ustedes/Ellos/Ellas (You all/They)	Ponen (You all/They put)	Pusieron (You all/They put)	Pondrán (You all/They will put)

Dormir (to sleep)

The verb 'Dormir' means 'to sleep'. The conjugation of 'Dormir' goes as follows:

Subject Pronouns	Present Tense	Past Tense	Future Tense
Yo (I)	Duermo (I sleep)	Dormí (I slept)	Dormiré (I will sleep)
Tú (You [informal])	Duermes (You sleep)	Dormiste (You slept)	Dormirás (You will sleep)
Usted/Él/Ella (You [formal]/He/She/It)	Duerme (You sleep or He/She sleeps)	Durmió (You/He/She slept)	Dormirá (You/He/She will sleep)
Nosotros [masculine]/Nosotras [feminine] (We)	Dormimos (We sleep)	Dormimos (We slept)	Dormiremos (We will sleep)

| Ustedes/Ellos/Ellas (You all/They) | Duermen (You all/They sleep) | Durmieron (You all/They slept) | Dormirán (You all/They will sleep) |

Now, let's explore stem-changing verbs.

Stem-changing Verbs

You may already know what stem is. If not, A stem refers to the part of the verb that comes before the ending of its infinitive form. For example, consider the infinitive verb 'Pensar' (to think). If you remove the ending 'ar', you are left with 'Pens__', and this remaining part is called the stem of the verb.

Some verbs undergo additional changes in their stems, known as stem-changing verbs. These changes usually are minor vowel changes such as:

- **e** changing to **ie**: p**e**nsar (to think) → p**ie**nso (I think)

- **o** changing to **ue**: m**o**ver (to move) → m**ue**vo (I move)

- **e** changing to **i**: m**e**dir (to measure) → m**i**do (I measure)

- **u** changing to **ue**: j**u**gar (to play) → j**ue**go (I play)

- **i** changing to **ie**: inqu**i**rir (to inquire) → inqu**ie**ro (I inquire)

The change occurs on the last syllable of the stem, regardless of how many other vowels are present in the verb. **These verbs are conjugated as regular verbs but with a stem change.** The stem changes similarly, regardless of whether the verb ends in -ar, -er, or -ir. **These stem changes happen in the present tense and do not affect the 'Nosotros' and 'Vosotros' forms.**

For example-

Let's consider the verb 'pensar' (to think).

Breakdown of the verb: *Pensar*

Stem: Pens__

*Stem-change: P**e**ns → P**ie**ns ('**e**' changes to '**ie**')*

The conjugation of 'Pensar' goes as follows:

Subject Pronouns	Present Tense	Past Tense	Future Tense
Yo (I)	P**ie**nso (I think)	Pensé (I thought)	Pensaré (I will think)
Tú (You [informal])	P**ie**nsas (You think)	Pensaste (You thought)	Pensarás (You will think)
Usted/Él/Ella (You [formal]/He/She/It)	P**ie**nsa (You think or He/She thinks)	Pensó (You/He/She thought)	Pensará (You/He/She will think)
Nosotros [masculine]/Nosotras [feminine] (We)	Pensamos (We think)	Pensamos (We thought)	Pensaremos (We will think)
Ustedes/Ellos/Ellas (You all/They)	P**ie**nsan (You all/They think)	Pensaron (You all/They thought)	Pensarán (You all/They will think)

For the second example,

Let's consider the verb 'Mover' (to move).

Breakdown of the verb: *Mov**er***

Stem: Mov__

*Stem-change: M**o**v → M**ue**v ('**o**' changes to '**ue**')*

The conjugation of 'Mover' goes as follows:

Subject Pronouns	Present Tense	Past Tense	Future Tense
Yo (I)	M**ue**vo (I move)	Moví (I moved)	Moveré (I will move)
Tú (You [informal])	M**ue**ves (You move)	Moviste (You moved)	Moverás (You will move)
Usted/Él/Ella (You [formal]/He/She/It)	M**ue**ve (You move or He/She moves)	Movió (You/He/She moved)	Moverá (You/He/She will move)
Nosotros [masculine]/Nosotras [feminine] (We)	Movemos (We move)	Movimos (We moved)	Moveremos (We will move)
Ustedes/Ellos/Ellas (You all/They)	M**ue**ven (You all/They move)	Movieron (You all/They moved)	Moverán (You all/They will move)

Here are some other common stem-changing verbs-

- Comenzar (to start)
- Concertar (to conclude)
- Probar (to try)
- Alentar (to encourage)
- Sosegar (to calm)
- Consolar (to comfort)
- Contar (to count)
- Costar (to cost)

- Acertar (to guess)
- Recordar (to remember)
- Aprobar (to approve)
- Renegar (to deny)
- Renovar (to renew)
- Asolar (to destroy)
- Resonar (to resonate)
- Desatender (to neglect)
- Entender (to understand)
- Demostrar (to demonstrate)
- Promover (to promote)
- Querer (to love/want)
- Sonreír (to smile)
- Doler (to hurt)
- Atender (to attend)
- Defender (to defend)
- Preferir (to prefer)
- Resolver (to solve)
- Discernir (to discern)
- Desenvolver (to unfold)
- Seguir (to follow)
- Repetir (to repeat)

Adverbs

An adverb **modifies/describes a verb**, **an adjective, or another adverb.** In English, many adverbs end in -ly, while in Spanish, **they often end in -mente.** Adverbs do not change according to the gender or number described in the sentence. They answer questions like how, when, and where.

In Spanish, **most adverbs can be formed simply by adding -mente to the end of the feminine or neutral adjective.** Neutral adjectives do not end in -o or -a but may end in -e, -l, -r, etc. They are neutral as they have one form to describe masculine and feminine nouns. Here's an example of forming adverbs out of adjectives-

Feminine adjective + mente

- Honesta (honest) + mente = honestamente (honestly)
- Perfecta (perfect) + mente = Perfectamente (perfectly)

Neutral adjective + mente

- Amable (kind) + mente = Amablemente (kindly)
- Igual (equal) + mente = Igualmente (equally)

The placement of adverbs depends on the word they are modifying. The adverb usually comes after the verb it modifies, but it may go before if it modifies another adverb or adjective.

Here's a list of some common adverbs:

Adverbs of Manner

- fácilmente (easily)
- usualmente (usually)
- normalmente (normally)
- generalmente (generally)

- frecuentemente (frequently)
- bien (well)
- mal (badly)
- perfectamente (perfectly)
- rápidamente (quickly)
- despacio (slowly)

For example-

- *Él lo hizo fácilmente. (He did it easily.)*
- *Él entendió perfectamente. (He understood perfectly.)*
- *Él camina despacio. (He walks slowly.)*
- *Ella terminó el trabajo rápidamente. (She finished the work quickly.)*

Adverbs of Time

- temprano (early)
- tarde (late)
- pronto (soon)
- ahora (now)
- ayer (yesterday)
- hoy (today)
- mañana (tomorrow)
- ya (already)
- todavía (still)

- siempre (always)
- a veces (sometimes)

For example-

- *Él llegó temprano. (He arrived early.)*
- *Él regresa pronto. (He returns soon.)*
- *Él salió ayer. (He left yesterday.)*
- *Él siempre ayuda. (He always helps.)*

Adverbs of Place

- aquí (here)
- allí/allá (there)
- cerca (near)
- lejos (far)
- arriba (up/above)
- abajo (down/below)
- afuera (outside)
- adentro (inside)

For example-

- *Ella está aquí. (She is here.)*
- *Ellos viven cerca. (They live nearby.)*
- *La tienda está lejos. (The store is far.)*
- *Los niños juegan afuera. (The kids play outside.)*

Adverbs of Quantity

- muy (very)
- poco (little/not much)
- más (more)
- menos (less/fewer)
- mucho (a lot/much)
- demasiado (too much)
- tan (so)
- tanto (so much)
- casi (almost)
- bastante (quite a bit/enough)
- suficiente (enough)
- todo (all/ everything)

For example-

- *Está muy frío. (It's very cold.)*
- *Hay poco tiempo. (There is little time.)*
- *Ella casi llega a tiempo. (She almost arrived on time.)*
- *Es suficiente. (It is enough.)*

Adverbs of Affirmation and Negation

- sí (yes)
- no (no)

- también (also)
- tampoco (neither)
- ciertamente (certainly)
- nunca/jamás (never)
- claro (of course/sure)
- apenas (hardly/barely)
- ningún (none)
- incluso (even)
- nada (nothing)
- nadie (nobody)

For example-

- *También quiero café. (I also want coffee.)*
- *Pues, claro. (Well, Of course.)*
- *No pasó nada. (Nothing happened.)*
- *Nadie vino. (No one came.)*

Adverbs of Doubt

- posiblemente (possibly)
- tal vez/quizás/a lo mejor (perhaps/maybe)
- realmente (really)
- seguramente (surely)
- probablemente (probably)

For example-

- *Posiblemente, este es el mejor restaurante de la ciudad. (This is possibly the best restaurant in town.)*

- *Tal vez venga mañana. (Maybe he will come tomorrow.)*

- *Seguramente lo encontrará. (Surely he will find it.)*

- *Probablemente ganen el partido. (Probably they will win the match.)*

The Gerund

The gerund is a verb form that indicates continuous or progressive actions. It corresponds to the '-ing' form in English. It does not change according to the gender or number. It is created by adding specific endings:

- **For -ar verbs:** The ending '-ando' is added. For example-
    - *Hablar (to talk) → Hablando (Talking)*
- **For -er and -ir verbs:** The ending '-iendo' is added. For example-
    - *Comer (to eat) → Comiendo (Eating)*
    - *Vivir (to live) → Viviendo (Living)*

If the 'er' and 'ir' verbs have a vowel at the end of the stem, you just add '-yendo.'

For example-

- *Leer (To read) → Leyendo (Reading)*
- *Oír (To hear) → Oyendo (Hearing)*

There is one key difference between English and Spanish gerunds. In English, the gerund can only refer to nouns, allowing phrases like **'Swimming is fun'**. However, **in Spanish, remember the gerund only refers to verbs. To refer to nouns in Spanish, you would use the infinitive form of the verb,** such as saying **'Nadar es divertido. (To swim is fun)'** to convey the same idea.

Now, let's review how gerunds are used.

Progressive Tenses: They are frequently used with the verb 'estar' to form progressive tenses, indicating an action happening at the moment of speaking.

For example-

- *Estoy **estudiando**. (I am **studying**.)*
- *Estoy **mejorando** mis habilidades de hablar. (I'm **improving** my speaking skills.)*

Describing Actions in Progress: They describe ongoing actions or situations.

For example-

- *Ella sigue **trabajando**. (She keeps **working**.)*
- *El reloj sigue **corriendo**. (The clock keeps **ticking**.)*

Simultaneous Actions: They can indicate actions that happen simultaneously with another action.

For example-

- *Estaba **leyendo** mi libro y María estaba **preparando** la cena. (I was **reading** my book and Maria was **preparing** dinner.)*
- *Juan estaba **trabajando** cuando empezó el terremoto. (Juan was **working** when the earthquake started.)*

Expressing Manner: They can describe how an action is performed.

For example-

- *Juan entró **corriendo** al cuarto. (Juan came **running** into the room.)*
- *Aprendí a nadar **flotando** en el agua. (I learned how to swim by **floating** in the water.)*

Past Participles

Past participles is also a verb form that often indicates a finished action. Regular past participles typically end in -ado or -ido. **To form regular past participles in Spanish, remove the -ar, -er, or -ir ending from an infinitive verb and add -ado for -ar verbs and -ido for -er or -ir verbs.**

For example-

- *Habl**ar** (To speak) → Habl__ → Habl**ado** (Spoken)*
- *Estudi**ar** (To study) → Estudi__ → Estudi**ado** (Studied)*
- *Com**er** (To eat) → Com__ → Com**ido** (Eaten)*
- *Beb**er** (To drink) → Beb__ → Beb**ido** (Drunk)*
- *Viv**ir** (To live) → Viv__ → Viv**ido** (Lived)*
- *Decid**ir** (To decide) → Decid__ → Decid**ido** (Decided)*

If the verb ends in a vowel after removing the -er or -ir ending of an infinitive verb, an accent mark is added to the 'i' making -ído to the ending.

For example-

- *Le**er** (To read) → Le__ → Le**í****do** (Read)*
- *Tra**er** (To bring) → Tra__ → Tra**í****do** (Brought)*

Irregular past participles, on the other hand, do not follow the same patterns. They usually end in -cho, -to, and sometimes -so. Here are the most common ones-

- Ver (To see) → Visto (Seen)
- Romper (To break) → Roto (Broken)
- Volver (To return) → Vuelto (Returned)

- Resolver (To resolve) → Resuelto (Resolved)
- Abrir (To open) → Abierto (Open)
- Morir (To die) → Muerto (Died)
- Escribir (To write) → Escrito (Written)
- Cubrir (To cover) → Cubierto (Covered)
- Decir (To say/tell) → Dicho (Said)
- Hacer (To do) → Hecho (Done/made)
- Poner (To put) → Puesto (Put)

Many of these irregular verbs mentioned above can be used as suffixes to form other verbs, such as des**cubrir** (to discover), contra**decir** (to contradict), des**hacer** (to undo), dis**poner** (to arrange/have), etc. Verbs formed using these suffixes will also have an irregular past participle. *For example-*

- *Descubrir (to discover) → Descubierto (Discovered)*
- *Contradecir (to contradict) → Contradicho (Contradicted)*
- *Deshacer (to undo) → Deshecho (Undone)*
- *Disponer (to arrange) → Dispuesto (Prepared)*

Some verbs can have both a regular and an irregular form of past participle. Such as-

Infinitive verb	Regular Participle	Irregular Participle
Corregir (To correct)	Corregido (Corrected)	Correcto (Correct)
Imprimir (To print)	Imprimido (Printed)	Impreso (Printed)
Soltar (To loosen/release)	Soltado (Released)	Suelto (Loose)

There are three main uses of past participle-

- To form perfect tenses
- To use as an adjective
- To form the passive voice

Forming Perfect Tenses

Forming perfect tenses in Spanish usually involves using the verb 'haber (to have)' followed by the past participle of the main verb.

Structure: ['haber' conjugated] + [past participle]

Let's first look at the conjugation of the verb 'haber':

Subject Pronouns	Present Perfect	Past Perfect	Future Perfect	Conditional Perfect
Yo (I)	He (I have)	Había (I had)	Habré (I will have)	Habría (I would have)
Tú (You [informal])	Has (You have)	Habías (You had)	Habrás (You will have)	Habrías (You would have)
Usted/Él/Ella (You [formal]/He/She/It)	Ha (You/He/She/It have)	Había (You/He/She/It had)	Habrá (You/He/She/It will have)	Habría (You/He/She/It would have)
Nosotros [masculine]/Nosotras [feminine] (We)	Hemos (We have)	Habíamos (We had)	Habremos (We will have)	Habríamos (We would have)

| Ustedes/Ellos/Ellas (You all/They) | Han (You all/They have) | Habían (You all/They had) | Habrán (You all/They will have) | Habrían (You all/They would have) |

Now, let's take the past participle of the verb 'comer (to eat)' as an example, which is 'comido', to form the perfect tenses below.

Present Perfect

- Yo **he comido.** (I have eaten.)
- Tú **has comido.** (You have eaten.)
- Usted/él/ella **ha comido.** (You/he/she have eaten.)
- Nosotros/nosotras **hemos comido.** (We have eaten.)
- Ustedes/ellos/ellas **han comido.** (You all/they have eaten.)

Past Perfect

- Yo **había comido.** (I had eaten.)
- Tú **habías comido.** (You had eaten.)
- Usted/él/ella **había comido.** (You/he/she had eaten.)
- Nosotros/nosotras **habíamos comido.** (We had eaten.)
- Ustedes/ellos/ellas **habían comido.** (You all/they had eaten.)

Future Perfect

- Yo **habré comido.** (I will have eaten.)
- Tú **habrás comido.** (You will have eaten.)
- Usted/él/ella **habrá comido.** (You/he/she will have eaten.)

- Nosotros/nosotras **habremos comido.** (We will have eaten.)
- Ustedes/ellos/ellas **habrán comido.** (You all/they will have eaten.)

Conditional Perfect

- Yo **habría comido.** (I would have eaten.)
- Tú **habrías comido.** (You would have eaten.)
- Usted/él/ella **habría comido.** (He/she/you would have eaten.)
- Nosotros/nosotras **habríamos comido.** (We would have eaten.)
- Ustedes/ellos/ellas **habrían comido.** (You all/they would have eaten.)

Using as Adjectives

When using past participles as adjectives, *ensure they reflect the gender and number of the nouns they describe.* The most common way to use past participles as adjectives is to use the verb 'estar (to be)' followed by the past participle. It can also be combined with other verbs.

Structure: [verb conjugated] + [past participle verb]

- La puerta **está cerrada**. (The door is closed.)
- Hoy me **siento** muy **cansada**. (I feel very tired today.)
- David **está obsesionado** con el dinero. (David is obsessed with money.)
- El coche **está reparado**. (The car is repaired.)

Forming the Passive Voice

The past participle plays a crucial role in creating the passive voice in Spanish. *It should agree with the subject in terms of gender and number.* To create the passive voice, use the verb 'ser' in the correct tense, followed by the past participle of the main verb.

Structure: ['ser' conjugated] + [past participle]

- Las cartas son escritas por David. (The letters are written by David.)

- El edificio fue construido en 1995. (The building was built in 1995.)

- El trabajo habría sido terminado si hubiéramos tenido más tiempo. (The work would have been finished if we had more time.)

Reflexive Verbs

Reflexive verbs are those where the subject performs an action on itself. They are accompanied by reflexive pronouns, which indicate that the verb's action is reflected back onto the subject. In English, pronouns such as myself, yourself, himself, and ourselves are used with verbs to denote reflection, whereas in Spanish, the following reflexive pronouns are used:

- me (myself)
- te (yourself [informal])
- se (himself, herself, itself, yourself [formal])
- nos (ourselves)
- se (themselves, yourselves [formal])

These pronouns come before the conjugated verb. It may also be attached to the end of an infinitive, gerund, or affirmative command.

Since the gerund is almost always paired with the verb 'estar,' the reflexive pronoun should come before 'estar' when unattached.

For example-

Unattached - **Me estoy** *lavando. (I'm washing)*

Attached - *Estoy lavándome. (I'm washing)*

Note: If you attach the reflexive pronoun to the end of the gerund, remember to include an accent mark on the third to last syllable, like in the above example, 'lav**á**ndome.'

The infinitive form of reflexive verbs always ends in -se. 'Se' means 'to oneself' and reflects on the person who performs the action. This suffix indicates that the verb is reflexive.

- lavar**se** (to wash)
- afeitar**se** (to shave)
- bañar**se** (to bathe)

- cepillar**se** (to brush)

To conjugate a reflexive verb, follow these simple steps:

- Identify the verb and its reflexive pronoun.
- Remove the -se ending from the infinitive form of the reflexive verb.
- Conjugate the verb as you would normally.
- Then add the reflexive pronoun before the conjugated verb.

For example: Lavarse (to wash oneself)

Remove the '-se' ending from the infinitive form of the reflexive verb 'Lavarse,' making it 'lavar.' Then, conjugate the verb as usual by replacing the '-ar' ending depending on its tense and subject.

- Yo me lavo. (I wash myself.)
- Tú te lavas. (You wash yourself.)
- Usted/él/ella se lava. (You/He/She washes yourself/himself/herself.)
- Nosotros/nosotras nos lavamos. (We wash ourselves.)
- Ustedes/ellos/ellas se lavan. (You all/They wash themselves/yourselves.)

Sentences

As in any language, sentences are essential for expressing thoughts, feelings, and ideas clearly and effectively. Whether you are ordering food at a restaurant, conversing with a friend, or asking for directions, understanding how sentences are constructed will enable you to communicate with confidence. So, let's dive in and unlock the world of Spanish sentences, paving the way for richer communication!

The most basic sentence structure in Spanish is 'Subject + Verb + Object'.

- The subject indicates who is performing the action
- The verb indicates the action itself
- The object indicates who or what the action is performed on.

For example-

Yazmin escribe un libro.

Here, **Yazmin** is the subject, **escribe (writes)** is the conjugated verb, and **un libro (a book)** is the object: **Yazmin writes a book.**

As you can see, the order is similar to the one used in English. However, there can be big differences between the two languages, and they do not always use the same formula. Spanish sentence structures are flexible. One of its beauties is that you can change the basic structure to emphasize different parts of your message. Variations such as 'Verb + Subject + Object (VSO)', 'Subject + Object + Verb (SOV)', or 'Object + Subject + Verb (OSV)' are used depending on the intended emphasis.

When using pronouns, adjectives, and adverbs in sentences, there are a few things you need to keep in mind. Below are some guidelines to remind you where each of them goes in a sentence-

- **Pronouns:** All types of pronouns go before the verb; however, if the verb is in the imperative, gerund, or infinitive form, the pronoun will go after the verb.

- **Adjectives:** Adjectives always go after nouns in Spanish.
- **Adverbs:** Different types of adverbs have different positions in a sentence.
  - Adverbs that modify adjectives come before the adjectives.

    For example- Soy **muy alto.** (I'm **very tall.**)

    In this example, the adverb 'muy (very)' modifies the adjective 'alto (tall).'
  - Adverbs that modify other adverbs also come before the adverbs they modify. For example - Puede correr **tan rápido.** (He can run **so quickly.**) In this example, the adverb 'tan (so)' modifies the other adverb 'rápido (quickly).'
  - Adverbs that modify a verb should come after the verb. For example- Él **corrió rápidamente**. (He **ran quickly**.) In this example, the adverb 'rápidamente (quickly)' modifies the verb 'corrió (ran).'
  - Adverbs of negation should come before the verb. For example- Él **no come** carne. (He **does not eat** meat.) In this example, the adverb 'no (does not)' conveys negation before the verb 'come (eat)'.

Now, let's explore the various types of Spanish sentences, such as declarative, negation, questions, indirect questions, and those involving direct and indirect object pronouns. Let's explore them one by one.

Declarative Sentences

Declarative sentences provide information about a particular event or situation and are usually used to talk about daily life.

Many times in Spanish, it is ***not necessary to add a subject, except if you want to emphasize who is doing the action:***

- *(Yo)* **Compro** *ropa.* (***I buy*** *clothes.*)
- *(Tú)* **Compras** *ropa.* (***You buy*** *clothes.*)
- *(Ellos)* **Compran** *ropa.* (***They buy*** *clothes.*)

Structure: Subject + conjugated verb + object

You will always have a conjugated verb that agrees in **person** and **number** with the omitted subject.

Negation Sentences

Negation sentences are used to deny a fact. They are the most straightforward form of sentences; *just add a 'no' before the verb.*

For example-

- *(Yo)* **No voy** *al cine.* (**I don't go** *to the cinema.*)
- *(Yo)* **No como** *salsa.* (**I don't eat** *salsa.*)

Structure: Subject + no + conjugated verb + object

'No' is a common adverb of denial used for 'not.' However, you can also replace the word 'no' with other adverbs of denial depending on the situation, such as 'Nunca/Jamás (never),' 'Ni (neither/nor),' 'Tampoco (either/neither),' 'nadie (nobody/no one),' 'nada (nothing),' and so on.

For example-

- *(Yo)* **Nunca** *hago ejercicio.* (**I never** *exercise.*)
- *(Yo)* **Nunca** *veo la televisión.* (**I never** *watch television.*)
- **Nadie** *fue a la fiesta.* (**Nobody** *went to the party.*)

Double Negatives

Double negatives refer to sentences that include two negative words, which are very common in Spanish. The purpose of it is to emphasize a point. It may not sound right when translated into English, but it is grammatically correct in Spanish.

For example-

- **No** *sabes* **nada**. *(You* **don't** *know* **nothing**.*)*

- ***No** me gusta **nada**. (I **don't** like **nothing**.)*

Structure: No + conjugated verb + adverbs of denial / indefinite pronoun + complement

Here are some common adverbs of denial, which I mentioned earlier, and indefinite pronouns to form double-negative sentences.

The common adverbs of denial are:

- No: no/not
- Ni: neither/nor
- Nunca/Jamás: never
- Tampoco: either/neither

The common indefinite pronouns are:

- Nada: nothing
- Nadie: nobody/no one
- Ningún, ninguno/ninguna: none/any/anyone

Before you form double-negative sentences, below are some rules you need to remember:

- Don't use more than one negative word before a verb except for 'nunca jamás (never ever)'.
- A double negative cannot be formed if there is an adverb of Denial or an indefinite pronoun before the verb.
- Don't use both positive and negative words in statements.

Questions

Asking questions in Spanish is easy. Just take an affirmative sentence, put an upside-down question mark at the beginning and a question mark at the end, and raise your intonation at the end.

- *¿Rebeca pinta arte? (Does Rebeca paint art?)*
- *¿Tu papá está en el trabajo? (Is your dad at work?)*

Another simple way to turn a sentence into a question is to add a comma after the statement and add a question tag word, such as 'no' or 'verdad,' inside the interrogation signs. These words can represent any English question tags, depending on the context, such as 'Isn't he/she/it?', 'Doesn't he/she?', 'right?' etc.

For example-

- *Rebeca pinta arte, ¿no? (Rebeca paints art, right?)*
- *Te gusta la arte, ¿verdad? (You like art, right?)*

These question tags are used to confirm information or seek agreement.

The above questions are normally 'yes' and 'no' questions. To obtain more specific information, you must use interrogative question words such as 'what,' 'who,' 'when,' 'whom,' and so on. Here is the list of all question words, along with their purpose, structure, and an example.

Interrogative question words	Purpose	Sentence Structures	Examples
¿Qué? (What?)	To inquire about things, actions, qualities, or events.	¿Qué + noun/conjugated verb?	¿Qué es eso? (What is that?)

¿Quién? / ¿Quiénes? **[Plural]** (Who?)	To inquire about people	¿Quién / Quiénes + conjugated verb?	¿Quién es ese? (Who is that?) ¿Quiénes son ellas? (Who are they?)
¿De quién? / ¿De quiénes? [Plural] (Whose?)	To ask about possession	¿De quién/quiénes + conjugated verb?	¿De quién es esta foto? (Whose photo is this?) ¿De quiénes son estas fotos? (Whose photos are these?)
¿Cuándo? (When?)	To inquire about time or dates	¿Cuándo + conjugated verb?	¿Cuándo es tu cumpleaños? (When is your birthday?)
¿Dónde? (Where?)	To inquire about location and places	¿Dónde + conjugated verb + determiner + noun?	¿Dónde están mis Zapatos? (Where are my shoes?)
¿Cuál? / ¿Cuáles? [Plural] (Which?)	To inquire about a specific choice or option.	¿Cuál / Cuáles + noun/conjugated verb + complement?	¿Cuál es tu carro? (Which one is your car?) ¿Cuáles prefieres, los tacos o las enchiladas? (Which one do you prefer, tacos or enchiladas?)

¿Por qué? (Why?)	To inquire about the reasons or causes.	¿Por qué + noun/conjugated verb + complement?	¿Por qué decidiste mudarte a México? (Why did you decide to move to Mexico?)
¿Cómo? (How?)	To inquire about the manner or way something is done. **Note**: When inquiring about 'How big/old/new [something] is' in Mexico, use '¿Qué tan grande/viejo/nuevo es [something]?, instead of '¿Cómo de grande/viejo/nuevo es [something]?' For example- ¿Qué tan grande es tu casa? (How big is your house?)	¿Cómo + conjugated verb?	¿Cómo estás? (How are you?)
¿Cuánto? [Masculine] / ¿Cuánta? [Feminine] (How much?)	To inquire about amounts.	¿Cuánto / Cuánta + noun + conjugated verb?	¿Cuánto cuesta la camisa? (How much does the shirt cost?) ¿Cuánta comida preparaste para la fiesta? (How much food did you prepare for the party?)

¿Cuántos? [Masculine plural] / ¿Cuántas? [Feminine plural] (How many?)	To inquire about quantities.	¿Cuántos / Cuántas + noun + conjugated verb?	¿Cuántos tacos quieres? (How many tacos do you want?) ¿Cuántas casas hay en tu calle? (How many houses are there on your street?)

Indirect Questions

Indirect questions are used to ask about something more indirectly or politely. These questions are embedded in another sentence. They look the same as declarative sentences, and there is no inversion, other changes, or the use of signs.

- No sé **por qué vamos ahí.** (I don't know **why we're going there**.)
- Dime **cuánto tardarás**. (Tell me **how long it will take.**)
- Me pregunto **si le gusta**. (I wonder **if she/he likes it.**)

Uses of 'Qué'

In Spanish, the word 'qué' has multiple uses. One of the first things you recently learned about 'qué' is that it means 'what' when asking questions. Below, you'll discover how 'qué' can be used in other contexts.

'Qué' with The Accent

1. Expressing surprise or emphasis.

   What: <u>What</u> a great team! (¡Qué gran equipo!)

   How: <u>How</u> exciting! (¡Qué emocionante!)

'Que' without The Accent

1. Linking ideas together or making comparisons.

That: This is the team that I support. (Este es el equipo que apoyo.)

Than: My team is better than yours. (Mi equipo es mejor que el tuyo)

2. Expressing wishes:

May: May God bless you. (Que dios te bendiga).

3. Expressing cause or consequence:

Because: I'm not going because it's cold. (No voy, que hace frío.)

That: Move a little to the left so that I can see. (Muévete un poco hacia la izquierda para que yo pueda ver.)

4. Giving an order or command:

Let: Let the games begin! (¡Que empiecen los juegos!)

5. Creating a phrase:

Verb+Que: Some verbs pair with 'Que' to make a phrase. Verbs like 'Tener', which means 'to have' or 'to possess', when paired with 'Que', means to be obligated or to need to do something.

Have to: I have to go/leave. (Tengo que irme.)

Lo Que

'Lo que' is used similarly to English's non-question word 'what'.

For examples-

- You know **what** I mean. Sabes **lo que** quiero decir.

- You know **what** I want. Tú sabes **lo que** quiero

- *What* I mean is ….. - **Lo que** quiero decir es …..
- *What* I want is ….. - **Lo que** quiero es …..
- *What* I want to do is …..- **Lo que** quiero hacer es …..
- *What* I need is …..- **Lo que** necesito es …..
- *What* I need to do is …..- **Lo que** necesito hacer es …..

You can also think of it as **'the thing that/which'**.

Exception: *When 'what' comes before an infinitive verb, use 'qué' with the accent rather than 'lo que.'*

For example-

- I don't know **what** to say. (No sé **qué** decir.)
- I don't know **what** to do. (No sé **qué** hacer.)
- I don't know **what** to buy. (No sé **qué** comprar.)
- I don't know **what** to eat. (No sé **qué** comer.)

Sentences involving Direct and Indirect Object Pronouns

Direct Object Pronouns

Direct object pronouns replace nouns that directly receive a verb's action. For instance, in the sentence 'I bought a guitar,' the phrase 'a guitar' is the direct object. The phrase 'a guitar' can be replaced with the direct object pronoun 'it', resulting in the sentence 'I bought it.' Now that you know what direct object and direct object pronouns are, let's move on to the pronouns in Spanish that represent direct object pronouns.

Singular Direct Object Pronouns

Subject Pronouns	Direct Object Pronouns
Yo (I)	**Me** (Me)
Tú (You)	**Te** (You)
Él (He)	**Lo [masculine]** (Him, it)
Ella (She)	**La [feminine]** (Her, it)
Usted (You [formal])	**Lo [masculine]/La [feminine]** (You [formal])

<u>Plural Direct Object Pronouns</u>

Subject Pronouns	Direct Object Pronouns
Nosotros [masculine]/Nosotras [feminine] (We)	**Nos** (Us)
Ustedes (You all)	**Los [masculine]/Las [feminine]** (You all)
Ellos [masculine]/Ellas [feminine] (They)	**Los [masculine]/Las [feminine]** (Them)

There are a few things you need to remember when placing direct object pronouns in a sentence. Let's review them below.

- ❖ If there is only one verb in the sentence, the direct object pronoun is placed before the conjugated verb. For example-

    Direct object: *Traigo una guitarra. (I bring a guitar.)*

    Direct object pronoun: *Lo traigo. (I bring it.)*

    Structure: Direct object pronoun (*Lo [it]*) + Conjugated verb (*traigo [I bring]*)

❖ When using a conjugated verb with an infinitive verb, there are two ways to place the direct object pronoun.

   The first structure involves placing the direct object pronoun before the conjugated verb like the above.

   Direct object: Quiero traer una guitarra. (I want to bring a guitar.)

   Direct object pronoun: **Lo** quiero traer. (I want to bring it.)

   Structure: Direct object pronoun (*Lo [it]*) + Conjugated verb (*quiero [I want]*) + infinitive verb (*traer [to bring]*)

   The second structure involves attaching the direct object pronoun directly to the end of the infinitive verb.

   Direct object: Quiero traer una guitarra. (I want to bring a guitar.)

   Direct object pronoun: Quiero traer**lo**. (I want to bring it.)

   Structure: Conjugated verb (*Quiero*) + infinitive verb (*traer*) + direct object pronoun (*lo [attached]*)

Let's move on to indirect objects and their pronouns.

Indirect Object Pronouns

Indirect object pronouns replace nouns that indirectly receive a verb's action. For instance, in the sentence 'I brought the guitar to Paul,' the phrase 'to Paul' is the indirect object. The phrase 'to Paul' can be replaced with the indirect object pronoun 'to him', resulting in the sentence 'I brought it to him.'

   Note: To identify an indirect object in a sentence, **simply ask yourself 'to whom' or 'for whom' the action is done**. It is common to use the preposition 'a' or the contraction 'al,' a shortened version of 'a' and 'el' in Spanish to indicate 'to' before the indirect object that refers to a person or an animal.

For example-

David le regaló una guitarra a Pablo. (David gave a guitar to Paul).

Now that you know what indirect object and indirect object pronouns are, let's move on to the pronouns in Spanish that represent indirect object pronouns.

Singular Indirect Object Pronouns

Subject Pronouns	Indirect Object Pronouns
Yo (I)	**Me** (to me)
Tú (You)	**Te** (to you)
Él (He)	**Le [masculine]** (to him/it)
Ella (She)	**Le [feminine]** (to her/it)
Usted (You [formal])	**Le [masculine/feminine]** (to you)

Plural Indirect Object Pronouns

Subject Pronouns	Indirect Object Pronouns
Nosotros [masculine]/Nosotras [feminine] (We)	**Nos** (to us)
Ustedes (You all)	**Les** (to you all)
Ellos [masculine]/Ellas [feminine] (They)	**Les** (to them)

The indirect object pronouns always come before the direct object pronouns.

For example-

*Te lo traigo. (I bring it **to you**)*

Structure: Indirect object pronoun *(Te [to you])* + direct object pronoun *(lo [it])* + conjugated verb *(traigo [I bring])*

Also, remember, **when using the indirect object pronouns 'le' or 'les' along with the direct object pronouns 'lo,' 'la,' 'los,' or 'las' in a sentence, the 'le' or 'les' changes to 'se'** for phonetic reasons.

For example-

***Se** lo di. (I gave it **to him**.)*

Structure: Indirect object pronoun *(Se [to him])* + direct object pronoun *(lo [it])* + conjugated verb *(di [I gave])*

Verbs that take Indirect Object Pronouns

Some verbs in Spanish take indirect object pronouns even though they may appear as direct object pronouns in English. It is often the case with verbs that describe communication, emotion, or indirect actions.

For example-

- ***Decir (to say/tell):** **Te** digo. (I tell you.)*
- ***Interesar (to interest):** **Le** interesa. (It interests him/her)*
- ***Gustar (to like):** **Me** gusta. (I like it.)*

Let's clarify the concept by taking the verb **'gustar.' This verb actually means 'to be pleasing to**.' For example, **'Me gusta' translates literally to 'It is pleasing to me.**' In this phrase, 'to me' is the indirect object pronoun. Therefore, in the Spanish version, **the indirect object pronoun 'me' is used to express 'I like it.'**

I hope this clarifies the concept of why some verbs in Spanish use indirect object pronouns, even when they may seem like direct object pronouns in English.

Here are some other verbs that function similarly and also require the use of indirect object pronouns-

- **Faltar (to lack/need)**

    Spanish: Me falta tiempo. (Time is lacking to me.)

    English: I lack time.

- **Importar (to matter/care)**

    Spanish: No le importa. (It doesn't matter to him/her.)

    English: He/She doesn't care.

- **Quedar (to remain/to be left)**

    Spanish: Nos quedan diez minutos. (Ten minutes are left to us.)

    English: We have ten minutes left.

- **Doler (to hurt)**

    Spanish: Me duele la cabeza. (The head hurts me.)

    English: I have a headache.

- **Sobrar (to be left over)**

    Spanish: Les sobra comida. (Food is left over to them.)

    English: They have food left over.

- **Parecer (to seem)**

    Spanish: Te parece una buena idea. (It seems a good idea to you.)

    English: You think it's a good idea.

Sentence Starters and Connectors

Lastly, here are some useful sentence starters and connectors to consider.

- Regarding/In reference to/In regards to - En cuanto a
- Since/because/now that/considering that/given that - Ya que
- While - Mientras
- Before - Antes
- After - Después
- As soon as - En cuanto
- As well as - Además de
- Unlike - A diferencia de
- Unless - A menos que
- However - Sin embargo
- Besides/Moreover/as well - Además
- In spite of - A pesar de
- Instead of - En vez de
- Even though - Aunque
- Judging by - A juzgar por
- I want to say/I mean - Quiero decir
- That's why - Por eso
- Maybe/perhaps - A lo mejor
- Therefore/hence - Por lo tanto

Exercise 5

Conjugation

Conjugate the following regular infinitive verbs in the simple present tense and fill the blank spaces based on each subject pronoun.

- Cantar - To sing
- Leer - To read
- Escribir - To write

Verb: Cantar (To sing)

- I sing - Yo _____
- You sing - Tú _____
- He sings - Él _____
- We sing - Nosotros/Nosotras _____
- They sing - Ellos/Ellas _____

Verb: Leer (To read)

- I read - Yo _____
- You read - Tú _____
- He reads - Él _____
- We read - Nosotros/Nosotras _____
- They read - Ellos/Ellas _____

Verb: Escribir (To write)

- I write - Yo _____

- You write - Tú _____

- He writes - Él _____

- We write - Nosotros/Nosotras _____

- They write - Ellos/Ellas _____

Exercise 5.1

The Gerund

Convert the following infinitive verbs into their gerund forms.

- Comer (to eat) - _____

- Hablar (to speak) - _____

- Ir (to go) - _____

- Leer (to read) - _____

- Vivir (to live) - _____

Exercise 5.2

Past participles

Convert the following infinitive verbs into their past participle forms.

- Hablar (to speak) - _____

- Comer (to eat) - _____

- Vivir (to live) - _____

- Escribir (to write) - _____

- Abrir (to open) - _____

Exercise 5.3

<u>Reflexive verbs</u>

Conjugate the following reflexive verbs in the present tense and fill in the blank spaces based on each subject pronoun.

- Levantarse (to get up)
- Lavarse (to wash oneself)
- Vestirse (to get dressed)

<u>*Verb: Levantarse (to get up)*</u>

- I get up - Yo me _____
- You get up - Tú te _____
- He gets up - Él se _____
- We get up - Nosotros/Nosotras nos _____
- They get up - Ellos/Ellas se _____

<u>*Verb: Lavarse (to wash oneself)*</u>

- I wash - Yo me _____
- You wash - Tú te _____
- He washes - Él se _____
- We wash - Nosotros/Nosotras nos _____
- They wash - Ellos/Ellas se _____

<u>*Verb: Vestirse (to get dressed)*</u>

- I get dressed - Yo me _____

- You get dressed - Tú te _____

- He gets dressed - Él se _____

- We get dressed - Nosotros/Nosotras nos _____

- They get dressed - Ellos/Ellas se _____

Exercise 5.4

Identify the reflexive pronouns for each sentence in Spanish.

- ____ evanto temprano. (I get up early.)

- ____ vestimos rápido. (We get dressed quickly.)

- ____ acuesta a las diez. (He/She goes to bed at ten.)

- ____ despiertan tarde. (They wake up late.)

- ____ lavas las manos. (You wash your hands.)

Exercise 5.5

Sentences

Arrange the following words into a correct and coherent sentence.

- comemos / siempre / Nosotros / juntos / el / domingo.

- español / muy bien / Marta / habla.

- habla / muy / rápido / El / profesor.

- Nosotros / en / una / casa / grande / vivimos.

[Note: Answers are on pages 212-219.]

Vocabulary

Now that the fundamentals have been covered, it is time to focus on expanding your vocabulary.

Titles and Relations

- Sir - Señor
- Ma'am - Señora
- Miss - Señorita
- Young or Young man/woman - Joven
- The boy - El chico/niño
- The girl - La chica/niña
- The brother - El hermano
- The sister - La hermana
- The siblings - Los hermanos
- The nephew - El sobrino
- The niece - La sobrina
- The brother-in-law - El cuñado
- The sister-in-law - La cuñada
- The cousin (male) - El primo
- The cousin (female) - La prima
- The son - El hijo
- The daughter - La hija

- The children - Los niños
- The father - El padre
- The mother - La madre
- The uncle - El tío
- The aunty - La tía
- The parents - Los padres
- The grandfather - El abuelo
- The grandmother - La abuela
- The grandson - El nieto
- The granddaughter - La nieta
- The family - La familia
- The boyfriend - El novio
- The girlfriend - La novia
- The husband - El esposo
- The wife - La esposa
- The neighbor (male) - El vecino
- The neighbor (female) - La vecina
- A respectful way to address an older man, aged 40+, who is not a professional or whose profession you are unsure of - **Don + *their first name***
- A respectful way to address an older woman, aged 40+, who is not a professional or whose profession you are unsure of - **Doña + *their first name***

- A respectful way to address someone who has completed a university degree, excluding engineering or architecture - **_Licenciado/Licenciada + their first name_** or just **_Licenciado/Licenciada_**

Profession

- Lawyer - Abogado/Abogada
- Artist - Artista
- Athlete - Atleta
- Firefighter - Bombero/Bombera
- Carpenter - Carpintero/Carpintera
- Cook/Chef - Cocinero/Cocinera
- Waiter/waitress - Mesero/mesera
- Electrician - Electricista
- Nurse - Enfermero/Enfermera
- Engineer - Ingeniero/Ingeniera
- Mechanic - Mecánico/Mecánica
- Doctor - Médico/Médica
- Office worker - Oficinista
- Journalist - Periodista
- Plumber - Plomero/Plomera
- Police officer - Policía
- Teacher - Profesor/Profesora
- Student - Estudiante

- Secretary - Secretario/Secretaria

To ask about the profession, you can say: ¿A qué te dedicas? (What do you do for a living?)

An easy format to answer that question would be 'Soy **type of profession**'.

For example-

- *Soy Médico/Médica. (I'm a doctor.)*
- *Soy Ingeniero/Ingeniera. (I'm an engineer.)*
- *Soy Abogado/Abogada. (I'm a Lawyer)*

If you are retired, you could say, '***Estoy jubilado/jubilada. (I'm retired)***'

Endearment Terms

- My son/daughter - Mijo/Mija (These terms are the shortened form of 'mi hijo' (my son) or 'mi hija' (my daughter).
- Little one - Chiquito/Chiquita
- My love - Mi amor
- My heart - Mi corazon
- Handsome/Beautiful - Guapo/Guapa

Expressing Likes and Dislikes

Verbs you can use to express likes and dislikes-

- Gustar (To be pleasing to/to be liked)
- Caer (To fall)
- Encantar (To enchant/love)
- Amar (To love [use to show deepest love])

- Querer (To want/love [use to show lighter connotation of love and care])

- Preferir (To prefer)

- Importar (To matter/to be important/to care about)

- Interesar (To interest/be of interest)

- Fascinar (To fascinate/captivate)

- Odiar (To hate/detest)

- Detestar (To detest/hate/loathe)

An easy format to Like/dislike something would be:

- I like _____. - Me gusta/gustan[plural] _____.

- I love _____. - Me encanta/encantan[plural] _____.

- I prefer _____. - Prefiero _____.

- I'm interested in _____. - Me interesa _____.

- I'm fascinated by _____. - Me fascina _____.

- I don't mind/care _____. - No me importa _____.

- I don't like _____. - No me gusta _____.

- I hate _____. - Odio/Detesto _____.

For example-

Expressing likes and dislikes for an inanimate object

- I like this car. - Me gusta este carro.

- I like that car. - Me gusta ese carro.

- I like these cars. - Me gustan estos carros.

- I like those cars. - Me gustan esos carros.
- I love this car. - Me encanta este carro.
- I love that car. - Me encanta ese carro.
- I love these cars. - Me encantan estos carros.
- I love those cars. - Me encantan esos carros.
- I prefer this car. - Prefiero este carro.
- I prefer that car. - Prefiero ese carro.
- I prefer these cars. - Prefiero estos carros.
- I prefer those cars. - Prefiero esos carros.
- I am interested in this car. - Me interesa este carro.
- I am interested in that car. - Me interesa ese carro.
- I am interested in these cars. - Me interesa estos carros.
- I am interested in those cars. - Me interesa esos carros.
- I am fascinated by this car. - Me fascina este carro.
- I am fascinated by that car. - Me fascina ese carro.
- I am fascinated by these cars. - Me fascina estos carros.
- I am fascinated by those cars. - Me fascina esos carros.
- I don't mind/care about this car. - No me importa este carro.
- I don't mind/care about that car. - No me importa ese carro.
- I don't mind/care about these cars. - No me importa estos carros.
- I don't mind/care about those cars. - No me importa esos carros.
- I don't like this car. - No me gusta este carro.

- I don't like that car. - No me gusta ese carro.
- I don't like these cars. - No me gustan estos carros.
- I don't like those cars. - No me gustan esos carros.
- I hate this car. - Odio/Detesto este carro.
- I hate that car. - Odio/Detesto ese carro.
- I hate these cars. - Odio/Detesto estos carros.
- I hate those cars. - Odio/Detesto esos carros.

Using pronouns

- I like it. - Me gusta.
- I like this. - Me gusta esto.
- I like that. - Me gusta eso.
- I like them. - Me gustan.
- I like these. - Me gustan estos.
- I like those. - Me gustan esos.
- I love it. - Me encanta.
- I love this. - Me encanta esto.
- I love that. - Me encanta eso.
- I love them. - Me encantan.
- I love these. - Me encantan estos.
- I love those. - Me encantan esos.
- I prefer this. - Prefiero esto.
- I prefer that. - Prefiero eso.

- I prefer these. - Prefiero estos.
- I prefer those. - Prefiero esos.
- I am interested in this. - Me interesa esto.
- I am interested in that. - Me interesa eso.
- I am interested in these. - Me interesa estos.
- I am interested in those. - Me interesa esos.
- I am fascinated by this. - Me fascina esto.
- I am fascinated by that. - Me fascina eso.
- I am fascinated by these. - Me fascina estos.
- I am fascinated by those. - Me fascina esos.
- I don't mind/care about this. - No me importa esto.
- I don't mind/care about that. - No me importa eso.
- I don't mind/care about these. - No me importa estos.
- I don't mind/care about those. - No me importa esos.
- I don't like it. - No me gusta.
- I don't like this. - No me gusta esto.
- I don't like that. - No me gusta eso.
- I don't like them. - No me gustan.
- I don't like these. - No me gustan estos.
- I don't like those. - No me gustan esos.
- I hate this. - Odio/Detesto esto.
- I hate that. - Odio/Detesto eso.

- I hate these. - Odio/Detesto estos.
- I hate those. - Odio/Detesto esos.

Expressing likes and dislikes to people

- I like you. Me caes bien. (This phrase literally means, 'You fall well on me.' However, you can use it to say you like someone as a friend.)
- I like you. - Me gustas. (Use this phrase to indicate that you like someone a little more than a friend.)
- I like him/her/it. - Me gusta or Me gusta él/ella.
- I like them - Me gustan.
- He likes her. - A él le gusta ella.
- He likes them. - A él le gustan.
- She likes him. - A ella le gusta el.
- She likes them. - A ella le gustan.
- He/she likes it. - A el/ella le gusta.
- I love you. - Te amo (It has a deep, romantic meaning and is mostly used in long-term romantic relationships, such as between a husband and wife.)
- I want/love you. - Te quiero (Mostly used among friends, family, and loved ones to express care and affection in a more casual or affectionate manner.)
- I love him. - Lo amo/Lo amo a él.
- I love her. - La amo/La amo a ella.
- I don't like you. - No me caes bien.
- I don't like him/her. - No me gusta él/ella.
- I hate you. - Te odio.

- I hate him. - Lo odio.
- I hate her. - La odio.
- I hate them. - Los odio

Love Expressions

- Would you like to hang out with me? - ¿Quieres salir conmigo? (Use this to say, 'Would you like to go on a date with me?')
- Would you be my boyfriend/girlfriend? - ¿Quieres ser mi novio/novia?
- Would you like to go out to dinner with me? - ¿Te gustaría ir a cenar conmigo?
- Are you free this weekend? - ¿Estás libre este fin de semana?
- What do you think of this place? - ¿Qué opinas de este lugar?
- Shall we go somewhere else? - ¿Vamos a otro lugar?
- You look beautiful. - Te ves preciosa.
- You are beautiful. - Tu eres preciosa.
- You are so cute (To girl). - Eres tan linda.
- You are so cute (To boy). - Eres tan lindo.
- You look very pretty. - Te ves muy bonita.
- You have a very enchanting/charming smile. - Tienes una sonrisa encantadora.
- You look great. - Te ves genial.
- That was a great evening. - Fue una gran noche.
- I will drive you home. - Voy a llevarte a tu casa.
- I'll call you. - Te llamaré.
- I miss you a lot. - Te extraño mucho.

- I'd love to see you again. - Me encantaría verte de nuevo.

Movie Related

- Do you want to go to the movies? - ¿Quieres ir al cine?
- The movie is good. - La película es buena.
- The movie was really great. - La pelicula estuvo realmente genial.
- The movie was really good. - La pelicula estuvo realmente buena.
- The movie was very good. - La película estuvo muy buena.
- The movie was very cool. - La película estuvo muy padre/chida.
- The movie was so, so. - La película estuvo más o menos.
- The movie is not good. - La película no es buena.
- There were no good movies to watch. - No había ninguna película buena que ver.

Restaurant

- Welcome - Bienvenido (To male)/Bienvenida (To female) & Bienvenidos/Bienvenidas (to multiple people)
- Do you have a table for [number of people] people? - ¿Tiene una mesa para _____ personas?
- I have a reservation. - Tengo una reservación.
- How many people are with you? - ¿Para cuántas personas es la mesa?
- Are you ready to order? - ¿Están listos para ordenar?
- Would you like me to take your order? - ¿Quiere que le tome su orden?
- Yes/No - Sí/No

- Could you bring me [food items], please? - ¿Me podrías traer _____, por favor?

- Without chili, please! - ¡Sin chile, por favor!

- Enjoy your meal. - Provecho

- Can I get you something? - ¿Puedo invitarte algo?

- Would you like something else? - ¿Desean algo más?

- Anything else? - ¿Algo más?

- Would you please bring me the dessert menu? - ¿Me podría traer el menú de postres?

- Can I have the bill, please? - ¿La cuenta, por favor?

- Bring me the check, please. - Tráigame la cuenta, por favor.

- Would you like to pay together or separately? - ¿Quieren pagar juntos o separados?

- Can we have the bill separately? - ¿Me puede dar la cuenta por separado?

- This one is on me. - Yo pago.

Ask/Request

An easy format to ask/request something would be:

- Would it be possible _____? - ¿Sería posible _____?

- Could you bring me _____, please? - ¿Me podrías traer _____, por favor?

- Could you give me _____, please? - ¿Me podrías dar _____, por favor?

- Give me _____, please. - Me das _____, por favor.

- Can you pass me _____, please? - ¿Me pasas _____, por favor?

For example-

- *Would it be possible <u>to change seats</u>? ¿Sería posible <u>de cambiar de asiento</u>?*

- *Could you bring me <u>some enchiladas</u>, please? - ¿Me podrías traer <u>unas enchiladas</u>, por favor?*

- *Could you give me <u>a glass of water</u>, please? - ¿Me podrías dar <u>un vaso de agua</u>, por favor?*

- *Give me <u>a coke</u>, please. - Me das <u>una coca</u>, por favor.*

- *Can you pass me <u>the salt</u>, please? - ¿Me pasas <u>la sal</u>, por favor?*

Asking/Offering Help

- Excuse me - Disculpe (formal)/Disculpa (informal)

- I need help! - ¡Necesito ayuda!

- Can you help me? - ¿Me puedes ayudar?

- In what thing can I help you? - ¿En qué te puedo ayudar?

- How can I help you? - ¿Cómo puedo ayudarte?

- Yes, with what? - Sí, ¿con que?

- I need help with _____. - Necesito ayuda con _____.

- I need help to/for _____. - Necesito ayuda para _____.

- Can I help you? - ¿Puedo ayudarte(informal)/ayudarle(formal)?

- Do you need help? - ¿Necesitas ayuda?

- I can help you. - Puedo ayudarte.

- I'll help you (formal) - Yo le ayudo.

Giving Thanks

- Thanks! - ¡Gracias!

- Thank you very much - Muchas gracias/Muchísimas gracias

- Thanks for _____. - Gracias por _____.
- Thanks for helping me - Gracias por ayudarme.
- My pleasure! - ¡Con gusto!
- It was a pleasure. - Fue un placer.
- It was nothing. - De nada.
- No reason to thank me! - ¡No hay por qué!

Place and Building Names

- The house - La casa
- The building - El edificio
- The factory - La fábrica
- The skyscraper - El rascacielos
- The convention center - El centro de convenciones
- The amphitheater - El anfiteatro
- The palace - El palacio
- The prison - La prisión
- The town hall - La Presidencia municipal
- The city hall - El palacio municipal
- The church - La iglesia
- The school - La escuela
- The pharmacy - La farmacia
- The hospital - El hospital

- The gym - El gimnasio
- The park - El parque
- The bus station - La estación de autobuses
- The train station - La estación de tren
- The metro station - La estación de metro
- The airport - El aeropuerto
- The stadium - El estadio
- The golf course - La cancha de golf
- The swimming pool - La alberca/piscina
- The theme park - El parque temático
- The amusement park - El parque de atracciones
- The museum - El museo
- The embassy - La embajada
- The apartment - El apartamento
- The hostel - El hostal
- The office - La oficina
- The post office - La oficina postal
- The restaurant - El restaurante
- The cafe - El café
- The bar/pub - El bar
- The barber - El barbero
- The beauty salon - El salón de belleza

- The town/city - La ciudad
- The village - El pueblo

Directions

- Right - Derecha
- Left - Izquierda
- Straight - Derecho
- Near - Cerca
- Far - Lejos
- In front of - En frente de
- In the back - Atrás
- Behind - Detras/atrás
- Between - Entre
- Next to/Beside - Al lado de
- Through/Across - A través de
- Around - Alrededor
- Under/Underneath - Abajo de
- Turn left - De vuelta a la izquierda
- Turn right - De vuelta a la derecha
- Go straight - Vaya derecho

Here are some easy formats to ask and give directions:

1) Where's the _____? - ¿Dónde está el/la _____?

For example-

- *Where's the <u>supermarket</u>? - ¿Dónde está el <u>supermercado</u>?*
- *Where's the <u>bank</u>? - ¿Dónde está el <u>banco</u>?*
- *Where's my <u>car</u>? - ¿Dónde está mi <u>coche/carro</u>?*

2) I need to go to the _____. - Necesito ir a el/la _____.

For example-

- *I need to go to the <u>supermarket</u>. - Necesito ir al <u>supermercado</u>.*
- *I need to go to the <u>bank</u>. - Necesito ir al <u>banco</u>.*
- *I need to go to the <u>police station</u>. Necesito ir a la <u>estación de policía</u>.*

Note: The 'al' above is the shortened form of 'a (to) + el (the)', indicating that the noun is masculine. It is shortened to avoid vowel sound clashes in Spanish, so 'a el' is replaced with 'al'.

3) How do I get to the _____? - ¿Cómo llego a el/la _____?

For example-

- *How do I get to the <u>supermarket</u>? - ¿Cómo llego al <u>supermercado</u>?*
- *How do I get to the <u>bank</u>? - ¿Cómo llego al <u>banco</u>?*
- *How do I get to the <u>police station</u>? - ¿Cómo llego a la <u>estación de policía</u>?*

4) Is there a _____ near here? - ¿Hay un/una _____ cerca de aquí?

For example-

- *Is there a <u>supermarket</u> near here? - ¿Hay un <u>supermercado</u> cerca de aquí?*
- *Is there a <u>bank</u> near here? - ¿Hay un <u>banco</u> cerca de aquí?*
- *Is there a <u>police station</u> near here? - ¿Hay una <u>estación de policía</u> cerca de aquí?*

5) Excuse me, do you know where the _____ is? - Disculpe, ¿sabe dónde está el/la _____?

   For example-

   - *Excuse me, do you know where the <u>supermarket</u> is? - Disculpe, ¿sabe dónde está el <u>supermercado</u>?*

   - *Excuse me, do you know where the <u>bank</u> is? - Disculpe, ¿sabe dónde está el <u>banco</u>?*

   - *Excuse me, do you know where the <u>police station</u> is? - Disculpe, ¿sabe dónde está la <u>estación de policía</u>?*

6) Is the _____ far from here? - ¿Está el/la _____ lejos de aquí?

   For example-

   - *Is the <u>supermarket</u> far from here? - ¿Está el <u>supermercado</u> lejos de aquí?*

   - *Is the <u>bank</u> far from here? - ¿Está el <u>banco</u> lejos de aquí?*

   - *Is the <u>police station</u> far from here? - ¿Está la <u>estación de policía</u> lejos de aquí?*

7) Go past the _____. - Pase el/la _____.

   For example-

   - *Go past the <u>supermarket</u>. - Pase el <u>supermercado</u>.*

   - *Go past the <u>bank</u>. - Pase el <u>banco</u>.*

   - *Go past the <u>police station</u>. - Pase la <u>estación de policía</u>.*

8) It's at the corner of this _____. - Está en la esquina de esta _____.

   For example-

   - *It's at the corner of this <u>supermarket</u>. - Está en la esquina de esta <u>supermercado</u>.*

   - *It's at the corner of this <u>bank</u>. - Está en la esquina de esta <u>banco</u>.*

- *It's at the corner of this <u>police station</u>. - Está en la esquina de esta <u>estación de policía</u>.*

9) The _____ is in front of the _____. - El/la _____ está en frente de el/la _____.

   For example-

   - *The <u>supermarket</u> is in front of the <u>bank</u>. - El <u>supermercado</u> está en frente del <u>banco</u>.*

   - *The <u>post office</u> is in front of the <u>library</u>. - La <u>oficina postal</u> está en frente de la <u>biblioteca</u>.*

   - *The <u>police station</u> is in front of the <u>park</u>. - La <u>estación de policía</u> está en frente del <u>parque</u>.*

Note: The 'del' above is the shortened form of 'de(of) + el(the)', indicating that the noun is masculine. It is shortened to avoid vowel sound clashes in Spanish, so 'de el' is replaced with 'del'.

10) The _____ is behind the _____. - El/la _____ está detrás de el/la _____.

    For example-

    - *The <u>parking lot</u> is behind the <u>supermarket</u>. - El <u>estacionamiento</u> está detrás del <u>supermercado</u>.*

    - *The <u>post office</u> is behind the <u>bank</u>. - La <u>oficina postal</u> está detrás del <u>banco</u>.*

    - *The <u>police station</u> is behind the <u>supermarket</u>. - La <u>estación de policía</u> está detrás del <u>supermercado</u>.*

11) The _____ is next to the _____. - El/la _____ está al lado de el/la _____.

    For example-

    - *The <u>restaurant</u> is next to the <u>supermarket</u>. - El <u>restaurante</u> está al lado del <u>supermercado</u>.*

    - *The <u>bank</u> is next to the <u>post office</u>. - El <u>banco</u> está al lado de la <u>oficina postal</u>.*

- *The <u>police station</u> is next to the <u>coffee shop</u>. - La <u>estación de policía</u> está al lado del <u>café</u>.*

12) The _____ is between the _____ and the _____. - El/la _____ está entre el/la _____ y el/la _____.

For example-

- *The <u>restaurant</u> is between the <u>supermarket</u> and the <u>bank</u>. - El <u>restaurante</u> está entre el <u>supermercado</u> y el <u>banco</u>.*

- *The <u>bank</u> is between the <u>post office</u> and the <u>supermarket</u>. - El <u>banco</u> está entre la <u>oficina postal</u> y el <u>supermercado</u>.*

- *The <u>store</u> is between the <u>pet store</u> and the <u>coffee shop</u>. - La <u>tienda</u> está entre la <u>tienda de mascotas</u> y el <u>café</u>.*

Other Direction-Related Phrases

- How long does it take to get to this place? ¿Cuánto tiempo toma llegar a este lugar?

- How do I get to the airport? ¿Cómo llego al aeropuerto?

- How can I get to the metro station? - ¿Cómo puedo llegar a la estación del metro?

- Can you tell me how to get to the shopping center? ¿Puede decirme cómo llegar al centro comercial?

- Is there a store nearby? ¿Hay alguna tienda cerca?

- Yes, there is one in the corner. Sí, hay una en la esquina.

- Can you tell me which is the closest transportation? ¿Me puede decir cuál es el transporte más cercano?

- The closest is the metrobus. El más cercano es el metrobus.

- You have to walk this entire street. Tienes que caminar toda esta calle.

- Yes, you can walk there. Sí, puedes llegar caminando.

- What's the name of this street? ¿Cuál es el nombre de esta calle?

- It is Paseo de la Reforma. Es Paseo de la Reforma.

- Is this place far from here? ¿Este lugar está lejos de aquí?

- No, you can walk there. No, puedes llegar caminando.

- By car, it takes half an hour. En carro toma media hora.

- You can get there by metro, metro bus, taxi, or Uber. Puedes llegar en metro, metrobus, taxi o Uber.

Shopping

- The shop - La tienda

- The department store - La tienda departamental

- The supermarket - El supermercado

- The market - El mercado

- Cash - Dinero/efectivo

- The cashier - El cajero/La cajera

- The customer - El cliente

- Shopping bag - La bolsa de la compra

- Shop assistant - El asistente

- Self-service - El autoservicio

- The credit/debit card - La tarjeta de crédito/débito

- The loyalty card - La tarjeta de fidelidad

- The coupon - El cupón

- The price tag - La etiqueta de precio

- The barcode - El código de barras
- Sale - La venta
- The escalator - La escalera mecánica
- The elevator - El elevador
- Open - Abierto
- Closed - Cerrado
- What time do they open? - ¿A qué hora abren?
- What time do they close? - ¿A qué hora cierras?
- Do you have _____ ? - ¿Tiene _____ ?
- How much does it cost? - ¿Cuánto cuesta?
- Can you give it to me cheaper? - ¿Me lo deja más barato?
- I want _____ - Quiero _____
- I don't want _____ - No quiero _____
- I'm just looking, thank you. - Solo estoy viendo, gracias.

Transportation

- The Car - El Carro/coche
- The motorcycle - La motocicleta
- The bicycle - La bicicleta
- The scooter - La patineta
- The bus - El autobús
- The taxi - El taxi

- The airplane - El avión
- The ship - El barco
- The train - El tren
- The station - La estación
- The road - La carretera
- The street - La calle
- The Driver's license - La licencia de manejar
- All aboard! - Todos a bordo!
- The flight - El vuelo
- The passport - El pasaporte
- The ticket - El boleto
- The airplane ticket - El boleto de avión
- The suitcase - La maleta
- The luggage - El equipaje
- Time of departure - Hora de salida
- To board - Abordar
- Delayed - Retrasado
- To take off - Despegar
- To land - Aterrizar
- The hotel - El hotel
- Vacations - Vaciones
- The main square - El zócalo (Zócalo refers to Mexico City's central main square.)

- Can I see your ticket? - ¿Puedo ver su boleto?

- Yes, here you go. - Sí, aquí tiene.

- I purchased my _____ ticket online. - Compré mi boleto de _____ online.

- I purchased my plane ticket online. - Compré mi boleto de avión online.

- Can I have your passport? - ¿Me permite su pasaporte?

- The flight will leave in one hour. - El vuelo saldrá en una hora.

- We will start to board in 10 minutes. - Empezaremos a abordar en 10 minutos.

- The plane will take off in ten minutes. - El avión despegará en diez minutos.

- You've arrived at your destination! - ¡Has llegado a tu destino!

- I have a reservation. - Tengo una reservación.

- What time is check-out? - ¿A qué hora es la salida?

- Where are you traveling to? - ¿A dónde viaja?

- I'm going to the city center. - Voy al centro

- How much is the fare? - ¿Cuánto cuesta el pasaje?

- How much does it cost from here to the center? - ¿Cuánto cuesta ir de aquí al centro?

- Where do I get off? - ¿Dónde me bajo?

- I'm in a bit of a hurry. - Tengo un poco de prisa.

- Could you take the fastest route, please? - ¿Podría tomar la ruta más rápida, por favor?

- Could you drive more slowly, please? - ¿Podría manejar más despacio, por favor?

- Could you stop at an ATM, please? - ¿Podría parar en un cajero automático, por favor?

- Where is the main square? - ¿Dónde está el Zócalo?

Household Terms

- The door - La puerta
- The doorbell - El timbre de la puerta
- El pasillo - The hallway
- The window - La ventana
- The floor - El piso
- The ceiling - El techo
- The wall - La pared
- The stairwell - El hueco de la escalera
- The roof - La azotea
- The attic - El ático
- The drainage - El sistema de drenaje
- The furniture - Los muebles
- The table - La mesa
- The pen - La pluma
- The paper - El papel
- The alarm clock - El despertador
- The chair - La silla
- The bookshelf - El estante
- The wardrobe - El guardarropa
- The storage closet - El armario de almacenamiento

- The clothes hanger - El gancho
- The drawer - El cajón
- The rug/carpet - La alfombra
- The mirror - El espejo
- The room - La habitación
- The bedroom - La recámara/El Cuarto
- The bed - La cama
- The bed sheet - La sábana
- The pillow - La almohada
- The pillowcase - La funda de almohada
- The blanket - La manta
- The living room - La sala
- The Sofa - La sofá
- The bookshelf - El librero
- The kitchen - La cocina
- The stove - La estufa
- The oven - El horno
- The plate - El plato
- The glass - El vaso
- The cup - La taza
- The knife - El cuchillo
- The fork - El tenedor

- The spoon - La cuchara

- The cutlery - Los cubiertos

- The faucet - La llave

- The kitchen sink - El fregadero

- The broom - La escoba

- The dustpan - El recogedor

- The trash - La basura

- The trash bin - El bote de basura

- The trash bag - La bolsa de basura

- The mop - El trapeador

- The bucket - La cubeta

- The brush - El cepillo

- The rag/cloth - El trapo

- The kitchen towel/kitchen cloth - La toalla de cocina/Trapo de cocina

- The rubber gloves - Los guantes de goma

- The sponge - La esponja

- The soap - El jabón

- Dish soap - Jabón para trastes

- Dish detergent - Detergente para platos

- The laundry detergent - El detergente para ropa

- The bathroom/toilet - El baño

- The toothbrush - El cepillo de dientes

- The toothpaste - La pasta de dientes
- The towel - La toalla
- The bathroom sink - El lavabo
- The bathtub - La bañera/tina
- The shower - La regadera
- The shower gel - El gel de baño
- The shampoo - El champú
- The toilet paper - El papel higiénico
- The hallway - El pasillo
- The front yard - El patio delantero
- The driveway - La entrada de coches
- The back yard - El patio trasero
- The garden - El jardín
- The lawn/grass - El pasto
- The flower - La flor
- The tree - El árbol
- The garden hose - La manguera de jardín
- The watering can - La regadera
- The shovel - La pala
- The rake - El rastrillo
- The ladder - La escalera
- The garage - El garaje

Electronics

- The electronics - La electrónica
- Electronic device - Dispositivo electrónico
- The television - La televisión
- The Computer - La Computadora
- The webcam - La cámara web
- The speaker - La bocina
- The cell phone - El Celular
- The Charger - El cargador
- Cell phone charger/Charger for cell phone - Cargador para celular
- Phone charger/Charger of phone - Cargador de teléfono
- The cable - El cable
- The USB hub - El concentrador USB
- The adaptor - El adaptador
- The power cable - El cable de energía
- The power button - El botón de encendido
- The power bank - El banco de energía
- The memory card - La tarjeta de memoria
- The memory card reader - El lector de tarjetas de memoria
- The external drive - La unidad externa
- The scanner - El escáner

- The music player - El reproductor de música
- The lamp - La lámpara
- The light - La luz
- Light bulb - Foco
- The air conditioner - El aire acondicionado
- The hair dryer - La secadora de cabello
- The vacuum cleaner - La aspiradora
- The iron - La plancha
- The television - La televisión (Tele in shortened form)
- The microwave - El horno microondas
- The refrigerator - El refrigerador
- The electric kettle - El hervidor eléctrico
- The toaster - La tostadora
- The blender - La licuadora
- The dishwasher - El lavaplatos
- The washing machine - La lavadora

Food

The fruits - Las frutas

- The plum - La ciruela
- The kiwi - El kiwi
- The peach - El durazno

- The cherry - La cereza
- The apple - La manzana
- The grapefruit - La toronja
- The grapes - Las uvas
- The watermelon - La sandía
- The pear - La pera
- The banana - El plátano
- The cantaloupe - El melón
- The lime - El limón
- The lemon - El limón amarillo
- The peach - El durazno
- The orange - La naranja
- The guava - La guayaba
- The mango - El mango
- The pineapple - La piña
- The papaya - La papaya
- The apricot - El chabacano
- The cranberry - El arándano
- The blueberry - La mora azul
- The raspberry - La frambuesa
- The blackberry - La zarzamora
- The strawberry - La fresa

- The pomegranate - La granada
- The fig - El higo
- The starfruit - La carambola
- The passion fruit - El maracuya
- The quince - El membrillo
- The plantain - El plátano macho

The vegetables - Las verduras

- The cauliflower - La coliflor
- The broccoli - El brócoli
- The mushroom - El champiñón
- The lettuce - La lechuga
- The parsley - El perejil
- The radish - El rábano
- The asparagus - El espárrago
- The peas - Los chicharos
- The cucumber - El pepino
- The cabbage - El col/repollo
- The corn - El elote
- The potato - La papa
- The tomato - El jitomate
- The zucchini - La calabacita
- The green beans - Los ejotes

- The peas - Los chicharos
- The beetroot - El betabel
- The carrot - La zanahoria
- The turnip - El nabo
- The sweet potato - El camote
- The celery - El apio
- The green onion - La cebollita cambray
- The chives - El cebollines
- The asparagus - El espárragos
- The spinach - La espinaca
- The lentils - Las lentejas
- The garlic - El ajo
- The ginger - El jengibre
- The onion - La cebolla
- The coriander leaves - El cilantro
- The beans - Los frijoles

Other Food-Related Terms

- The meat - La carne
- The chicken - El pollo
- The fish - El pescado
- The beef - La carne de res
- The lamb - El cordero

- The pork - La carne de puerco
- The shrimp/prawn - El camarón
- The salt - La sal
- The black pepper - La pimienta negra
- The chilli powder - El chile en polvo
- The turmeric powder - La cúrcuma en polvo
- The curry powder - El curry en polvo
- The tortilla - La tortilla
- The rice - El arroz
- The cheese - El queso
- The sauce/salsa - La salsa
- The bread - El pan
- The water - El agua
- The coffee - El café
- The cake - El pastel
- The coke - La coca
- The ice-cream - La nieve
- The juice - El jugo
- The straw - El popote
- The Hot Dog - El hot dog/jocho
- The sandwich - La torta

- The tamale - El tamal (A traditional Mexican dish made with a corn-based dough mixture that is filled with various meats or beans and cheese)

- The Pozole - El pozole/posole (A thick, stewlike soup of pork or chicken)

- The enchilada - La enchilada (A folded tortilla filled with meat or cheese and covered with spicy sauce)

Taste

- Sweet - Dulce
- Salty - Salado
- Sour - Agrio
- Bitter - Amargo
- Spicy - Picoso/Enchiloso/Picante
- Sweet and sour - Agridulce
- Tasty - Sabroso/Sabrosa
- Bland - Desabrido/Desabrida
- Delicious - Delicioso/Deliciosa

To ask about the flavor/taste, you can say: ¿Qué sabor tiene? (What flavor does it have?)

An easy format to answer that question will be 'Está <u>type of taste</u>.'

For example-

- *Está dulce. (It's sweet.)*
- *Está salado. (It's salty.)*
- *Está picoso. (It's spicy.)*
- *Está delicioso. (It's delicious.)*

Clothes and Accessories

- High heels - Zapatos de tacón/Tacones
- The belt - El cinturón
- The blouse - La blusa
- The bra - El bra
- The coat - El abrigo
- The dress - El vestido
- The handbag - La bolsa de mano
- The hat - El sombrero
- The hoodie - La sudadera
- The jacket - La chamarra
- The Jeans - Los jeans
- The pajamas - La pijama
- The pants - Los pantalones
- The scarf - La bufanda
- The shirt - La camisa
- The shoelace - La agujeta
- The shoes - Los zapatos
- The shorts - Los shorts/Los pantalones cortos
- The skirt - La falda
- The slippers - Las pantuflas

- The socks - Los calcetines
- The suit - El traje
- The sweater - El suéter
- The underwear (In general) - La ropa interior
- The watch - El reloj
- Spectacles - Lentes de ver
- Sunglasses - Lentes de sol
- Contact lens - Lentes de contacto

Ornaments

- The jewelry - La joyería
- The necklace - El collar
- The ring - El anillo
- The bracelet - La pulsera
- The earrings - Los aretes

Colors

- The colors - Los colores
- Blue - Azul
- Red - Rojo/Roja
- Green - Verde
- Yellow - Amarillo/Amarilla
- White - Blanco/Blanca

- Black - Negro/Negra
- Pink - Rosa
- Purple - Morado/Morada
- Orange - Naranja or Anaranjado/Anaranjada
- Gray - Gris
- Brown - Café/Marrón

Terms to Describe Color

- Light/clear - Claro/Clara
- Dark/without light - Oscuro/Oscura
- Colorful - Colorido/Colorida
- Bright/shiny - Brillante
- Dull - Opaco/Opaca
- Transparent - Transparente

When discussing the color of something, you normally use the verb 'ser' as it's typically permanent; however, if the color is temporary, use the verb 'estar'.

For example,

Using 'ser'-

- *The shirt is red. - La camisa es roja.*
- *The shirts are red. - Las camisas son rojas.*

Using 'estar'-

- *The sky is gray. - El cielo está gris.*
- *The traffic light is green. - El semáforo está verde.*

To ask about the color, you could say-

- What's your favorite color? - ¿Cuál es tu color favorito?
- What's your preferred color? - ¿Cuál es tu color preferido?

To answer the above questions, you could say-

- My favorite color is blue. - Mi color favorito es el azul.
- My preferred color is orange. - Mi color preferido es el naranja.

Here's the simple format you can use-

- My favorite color is [The name of the color]. - Mi color favorito es el _____.
- My preferred color is [The name of the color]. - Mi color preferido es el _____.

Note: It is always masculine when referring to color as a noun.

Now, if you'd like to say a light or dark color, just add claro/oscuro after the color's name.

For example -

- *My favorite color is dark blue. - Mi color favorito es el azul oscuro.*
- *My preferred color is light orange. - Mi color preferido es el naranja claro.*

Body

- The ankle - El tobillo
- The arm - El brazo
- The back - La espalda
- The bald/Someone with little hair - Pelón
- The body - El cuerpo
- The chest/breast - El pecho

- The ears - Las orejas
- The elbow - El codo
- The eyes - Los ojos
- The feet - Los pies
- The fingers - Los dedos
- The hands - Los manos
- The head - La cabeza
- The heart - El corazón
- The knees - Las rodillas
- The legs - Las piernas
- The lips - Los labios
- The mouth - La boca
- The neck - El cuello
- The nose - La nariz
- The rib - La costilla
- The shoulder - El hombro
- The skin - La piel
- The stomach - El estómago
- The teeth - Los dientes
- The wrist - La muñeca

Animals

- The bear - El oso
- The bird - El pájaro
- The buffalo - El búfalo
- The bull - El toro
- The cat - El gato
- The cow - La vaca
- The crocodile - El cocodrilo
- The dog - El perro
- The donkey - El burro
- The duck - El pato
- The elephant - El elefante
- The fish - El pez
- The frog - La rana
- The goat - La cabra
- The hen - La gallina
- The horse - El caballo
- The lion - El león
- The monkey - El mono
- The mouse - El ratón
- The pig - El cerdo

- The rabbit - El conejo
- The rooster - El gallo
- The sheep - La oveja
- The snake - La serpiente
- The tiger - El tigre
- The turkey - El pavo
- The turtle - La tortuga
- The wolf - El lobo

Versatile Words

Here are some words that can have multiple meanings depending on the context.

Ándale: 'Ándale' is an informal Mexican term used to urge someone to move quicker or express agreement, frustration, or surprise.

- Come on
- Hurry up
- Awesome
- Go on/Continue
- Ok
- I see/understand
- Let's go
- Geez

Órale: 'Orale' is a slang term Mexicans use to express admiration, agreement, surprise, approval, or disappointment. It can also serve as a prompt to encourage someone to take action.

- Bring it on!
- Come on!
- Exhortation
- Go ahead
- Hurry up
- I agree with you
- I'm flabbergasted
- I'm waiting for you
- It's your turn
- Ok
- That's amazing
- There you go
- Watch it
- Yeah
- Wow

Pedo/Peda: 'Pedo' literally means 'fart' in Spanish. It is commonly used in Mexico to mean drunk, party, problem, etc, depending on the context. Here are some examples:

- What's up?/ What's your problem? (Depending on the tone) - ¿Qué pedo? (Just use it between your friends)
- I got drunk. - Anoche me puse pedo.

- No worries/no problem. - No hay pedo.
- To be idle/have nothing to do. - Estoy al pedo.
- Where's the party? - ¿Dónde es la peda?
- I'm drunk. - Estoy/ando bien pedo.
- I really got drunk. - Me puse bien pedo.
- He's very drunk. - Él está bien pedo.
- She's very drunk. - Ella está bien peda.
- We have problems - Tenemos pedos.
- You always get into problems - Tú siempre te metes en pedos.
- Here's no trouble - Aquí no hay pedo.
- That sucks - Qué mal pedo.
- It's all bullshit/you're lying - Puro pedo.

Claro/Clara: 'Claro' is used to express emphasis, agreement, or describe something.

- Of course!
- You're right
- I understand
- Sure
- Clear
- Light

Sale: 'Sale' is used to agree with something.

- Ok
- Yeah

- Sure
- Cool

Cochino/Cochina: The literal meaning is pig, but it can also be used metaphorically. It's a term with a negative connotation. For example - ¡No seas cochino! (Don't be a pig!)

- Dirty
- Gross
- Messy
- Nasty
- Pervy

Ways to Start a Conversation

Let's now look at some common ways to start a conversation.

Greetings will be, as Mexicans like to say, your bread of every day. The ones that you use are:

- Buenos días - Good morning
- Buenas tardes - Good afternoon
- Buenas noches - Good night

As you can see, all three have the word 'buenos' at the beginning. This is the plural of 'bueno,' which means **good**. They are used as greetings in all contexts but can also be used in different situations, for example:

You wake up later than usual and arrive late to a gathering. Your Mexican friends could say to you: ¡Buenas noches! Which, in this context, implies that you are so late that it could be night already.

Also, it is important to remember that 'buenas noches' can mean 'sleep well' or 'have a good night.'

Some other phrases that you will hear are:

- Mucho gusto - Nice to meet you.
- Encantado/Encantada de conocerte - Is my pleasure meeting you.
- ¿Cómo estás? - How are you?
- ¿Cómo va todo? - How's everything going?
- ¡Qué gusto verte! - Is nice meeting you!

These words are usually the starters of a conversation, so you will hear them quite often. Now, answering most of them is as easy as it sounds. I'll give you an example of how a conversation would go:

- *¡Buenos días! ¿Cómo estás? (Good morning! How are you?)*

- *¡Buenos días! Muy bien, ¿y tú? (Good morning. Fine, and you?)*

- *¡Bien, gracias! ¡Qué gusto verte! (Fine, thank you. Is nice meeting you!)*

- *¡Igualmente! ¿Cómo va todo? (Likewise. How is everything going?)*

- *Bien, gracias por preguntar. Recuérdame, ¿cuál es tú nombre? (Good, thank you for asking. Tell me again, what is your name?)*

- *Mi nombre es Jacob. (My name is Jacob.)*

- *Gracias, Jacob. Dime, ¿de dónde eres? (Thank you, Jacob. Tell me, where are you from?)*

- *Soy de Inglaterra. (I am from England.)*

This conversation can be set, for example, at a resort club where you want to join some activities or at the lobby of the hotel to ask for any type of information.

Another example of a fairly common conversation is the one you might have when checking in at a hotel:

- *¿Cuántas personas lo acompañan? (How many people travel with you?)*

- *Somos cinco personas. (We are five.)*

- *Muy bien, ¿cuántas habitaciones necesitan? (Very well, how many rooms do you need?)*

- *Queremos tres habitaciones, por favor. (We want three, please.)*

- *¿Viaja algún menor de edad con ustedes? (Is there any minor in your group?)*

- *No, todos somos adultos. (No, we are all adults.)*

- *Muy bien, aquí tiene sus llaves. (Very good, here are your keys.)*

Now, what about a more normal daily conversation? Let's say it's your first day in Mexico City, and your friend mentions the weather. The conversation would be something like this:

- *¡Hola, Jacob! ¿Cómo va tu día? (Hello, Jacob! How's your day going?)*

- *¡Hola, Mateo! Muy bien, ¿qué tal el tuyo? (Hello, Mateo. Fine, and yours?)*

- *¡Terrible! Empezó a llover cuando salí de casa. (Terrible! It started raining when I went out.)*

- *¿En serio? En donde yo vivo estaba soleado. (Really? Where I live was very sunny.)*

- *¡Qué envidia! ¿Prefieres días lluviosos o soleados? (How nice! Do you prefer rainy days or sunny days?)*

- *¡Soleados! En Inglaterra casi siempre está nublado. (Sunny! In England, almost every day is cloudy.)*

- *Ya veo. ¿No te molesta el calor? (I see. You don't get bothered by the heat?)*

- *¡Para nada! ¡Me gusta mucho! (Not really! I like it very much!)*

The weather in Mexico, specifically in Mexico City, can change from one moment to the next, and it also depends on where in the city you are. That's why you should learn these important words.

- Lluvia - Rain
- Soleado - Sunny
- Frío - Cold
- Templado - Temperate
- Sol - Sun
- Granizo - Hail
- Inundación - Flood
- Nublado - Cloudy

An easy format to say how the weather is today would be: Hoy está (type of weather).

For example:

- *Hoy está soleado. (Today is sunny.)*

- *Hoy está lloviendo. (Today is raining.)*
- *Hoy está nublado. (Today is cloudy.)*
- *Hoy granizó. (Today it hailed.)*
- *Hoy se inundó. (Today it flooded.)*
- *Hoy hace frío. (Today is cold.)*

After talking about the weather, your friend invited you to eat together with his other friends:

- *¿Qué te gustaría comer, Jacob? (What would you like to eat, Jacob?)*
- *¿Qué opciones de comida hay? (What food options are there?)*
- *Hay restaurantes mexicanos, italianos y japoneses. Puedes elegir el que quieras. (There are Mexican, Italian, and Japanese restaurants. You can choose whatever you want.)*
- *Quisiera comer comida mexicana. (I would like to eat Mexican food.)*
- *Muy bien, ¿quieres tacos o antojitos? (Very good, would you like tacos or antojitos?)*
- *Quiero probar los antojitos, ¿qué son? (I would like to try antojitos, what are they?)*
- *Son una mezcla de muchas cosas, podemos mostrarte. (They are a mix of many things, we can show you.)*
- *¿Saben bien? (Do they taste good?)*
- *Sí, no te vas a arrepentir. (Yes, you won't regret it.)*
- *Muy bien, ¡vamos! (Very well, let's go!)*

When you finish eating, you need to go back to your residence. Your friend offers to drive you there, but you want to walk around and get to know the city:

- *¿Quieres que te llevemos a tu casa? (Do you want us to drive you home?)*
- *No, gracias, quiero ir a caminar. (No, thank you, I would like to walk.)*

- *Bueno, ¿sabes cómo regresar? (Ok, do you know how to go back?)*
- *No estoy muy seguro, ¿qué opciones hay? (I'm not sure, what options are there?)*
- *Puedes usar el metro, el metrobus, pedir un taxi o rentar una bicicleta. (You can take the metro, metrobus, ride a taxi, or rent a bicycle.)*
- *¿Cómo puedo usar el metro? (How can I take the metro?)*
- *Necesitas comprar una tarjeta y el viaje cuesta cinco pesos. (You need to buy a card, and the ride is five pesos.)*
- *Gracias, creo que esta vez usaré esa opción. (Thank you, I think I will use that option.)*
- *La estación más cercana está a dos cuadras. (The closest station is two blocks away.)*
- *Bien, gracias. ¡Nos vemos mañana! (Well, thank you. See you tomorrow!)*

Note: Most forms of transportation in Mexico use a card called the **'Tarjeta de movilidad integrada' (Integrated Mobility Card),** which can be easily purchased at any metro or Metrobus station and recharged using your phone.

When buying a metro card at a station, the conversation usually goes like this:

- *Hola, quiero comprar una tarjeta para el metro. (Hello, I want to buy a metro card.)*
- *Hola, sí, claro. Cuesta $15 pesos. (Hi, yes, of course. It costs $15 pesos.)*
- *Aquí tiene, muchas gracias. (Here you go, thank you very much.)*
- *¿Para qué puedo usar mi tarjeta de movilidad integrada? (What can I use my integrated mobility card/metro card for?)*
- *Puedes usarla para el metro, el metrobus, las eco-bicis, el trolebús, el cablebus y el tren ligero. (You can use it for the metro, metrobus, eco-bikes, trolleybus, cablebus and light rail.)*
- *¿Dónde puedo recargarla? (Where can I recharge it?)*
- *En cualquier maquina o taquilla de las estaciones de metro y metrobus. (In any machine or ticket office in the metro and metrobus stations.)*

Now, to recharge the card:

- *Hola, quiero cargar dinero a mi tarjeta. (Hello, I want to charge money to my card.)*
- *Hola, sí claro. ¿Cuánto quieres cargar? (Hi, yes of course. How much do you want to charge?)*
- *¿Cuánto cuesta un viaje ida y vuelta? (How much does a round trip cost?)*
- *¿Un viaje de metro o de metrobus? (A metro or metrobus trip?)*
- *De metro, por favor. (From the subway, please.)*
- *El precio del metro es de $10 pesos. (The subway price is $10 pesos.)*
- *¿Cuánto cuesta el viaje en metrobus? (How much does the metrobus trip cost?)*
- *El de metrobus es de $12 pesos. (The metrobus costs $12 pesos.)*
- *Bien, quiero cargar $50 pesos, por favor. (Okay, I want to charge $50 pesos, please.)*

Other Useful Terms and Phrases

- Hello - Bueno (Bueno means Good/well, but it is also used to say 'hello' in Mexico when answering the phone)
- How was your day/How's your day going? - ¿Qué tal tu día?
- Have a good time. - Qué la pases bien.
- Take care. - Cuídate
- Bye - Bye/Adiós
- It's a pleasure to meet you! - ¡Un gusto conocerte!
- It was nice to see you(formal). - Fue un gusta verle.
- Lovely to meet you. - Encantado de conocerte.
- Nice to meet you - Mucho gusto

- I'd love to see you again. - Me encantaría verte de nuevo.

- Bye, see you! - ¡Chao, nos vemos!

- See you later - ¡Hasta luego!

- Have a good day. - Que tengas un buen día.

- How old are you? - ¿Qué edad tienes?

- When is your birthday? - ¿Cuándo es tu cumpleaños?

- My birthday is on the 19th of February. - Mi cumpleaños es el nineteen de febrero.

- How do you like to celebrate it?- ¿Cómo te gusta celebrar?

- Going to a party. - Yendo de fiesta.

- What do you do for a living? - ¿A qué te dedicas?

- I am a musician. - Soy música.

- Where are you from? - ¿De dónde eres?

- I'm from the UK. - Soy del Reino Unido.

- What is your favorite sport? - ¿Cuál es tu deporte favorito?

- I like soccer. - A mí me gusta el soccer.

- Why do you like soccer? - ¿Por qué te gusta el soccer?

- Because it is fun. - Porque es divertido.

- Which day of the week do you exercise? - ¿Qué día hacer ejercicio?

- I exercise all week. - Hago ejercicio toda la semana.

- Do you practice a sport, or do you go to the gym? - ¿Practicas un deporte o vas al gimnasio?

- I go to the gym. - Voy al gimnasio.

- Do you have brothers? - ¿Tienes hermanos?
- No, I just have sisters. - No, solo tengo hermanas.
- How many do you have? - ¿Cuántas hermanas tienes?
- I have two younger sisters. - Tengo dos hermanas menores.
- Do you like going shopping? - ¿Te gusta ir de compras?
- Not really. - No mucho.
- Why? - ¿Por qué?
- I think it is boring. - Creo que es aburrido.
- Do you like going to the movies? - ¿Te gusta ir al cine?
- Yes, I like it very much. - Sí, me gusta mucho.
- What is your favorite movie? - ¿Cuál es tu película favorita?
- I like 'Titanic'. - Me gusta 'Titanic'
- Do you prefer hot or cold? - ¿Prefieres el calor o el frío?
- I prefer the cold. - Prefiero el frío.
- When it is cold, do you drink coffee or tea? - Cuando hace frío, ¿tomas café o té?
- I drink tea. - Tomo té.
- What is your favorite dessert? - ¿Cuál es tu postre favorito?
- The strawberry cake. - Es el pastel de fresa.
- Do you eat it often? - ¿Lo comes seguido?
- Yes, whenever I can. - Sí, siempre que puedo.
- Friend - Amigo/Amiga
- Someone - Alguien

- Something/Anything - Algo
- Like this/Like that - Así
- Tell me - Dime
- Let's see - A ver (It is used to pause, think, or express uncertainty in a conversation.)
- Come/Watch - Ven
- Stop - Para
- Go - Ve
- Wait - Espera
- Yeah, right - Si, claro.
- Oh, yeah - Ay, ya
- Ok - Va/Sale
- Pardon? - ¿Mande?
- Please - Por favor
- Sorry - Perdón
- I'm sorry. - Lo siento (It literally means 'I feel it,' but it's another way to say sorry.)
- Forgive me. - Perdóname
- I forgive you. - Te perdono
- You're forgiven. - Estás perdonado
- Don't worry about it. - No pasa nada
- No worries - No hay problema
- To be far away - Estar relejos
- Do you know what I'm feeling? - ¿Sabes lo que siento?

- You know what I'm feeling. - Tú sabes lo que siento.

- What happened? - ¿Qué pasó?

- I didn't see you. - No te vi.

- What's happening?/What's going on? - ¿Qué pasa?

- I can't hear you. No te escucho.

- We are not ready yet. - Todavía no estamos listos

- I'll wait for another one. - Esperaré otro.

- Guess what? - ¿Adivina qué?

- What do you think? - ¿Que crees?

- What's new? - ¿Qué novedades? (Without a question mark, it would mean 'What a novelty/surprise!'.)

- What do you have? - ¿Qué tienes?

- What are you looking for? - ¿Qué buscas?

- What do you want? - ¿Qué quieres?

- What do you want to accomplish? - ¿Qué quieres lograr?

- Well/so - Pues (The shortened version of 'pues' is 'pos')

- What a surprise! - ¡Qué sorpresa!

- I can't believe it! - ¡No puedo creerlo!

- Alright/Ok - Sale

- I'd love to! - Me encantaría

- Likewise/Same to you/Equally - Igualmente

- Really/Seriously? - ¿Al chile?

- Is it free? - ¿Es gratis?
- I don't know. - No sé.
- I'm not sure - No estoy seguro.
- Well, let me think - Pues, déjame pensar
- Well, now you're ready! - ¡Pos, ahora estás listo!
- Could you do this, please? - ¿Podrías hacer esto, por favor?
- Do you accept card payments? - ¿Acepta pagos con tarjeta?
- Do you accept credit card? - ¿Aceptan tarjeta de crédito?
- No, only cash. - No, solo efectivo.
- I'm sorry, I don't speak Spanish. - Lo siento, no hablo español.
- Do you speak English by any chance? - ¿Hablas inglés, de casualidad?
- I don't understand. - No entiendo.
- Could you speak more slowly, please? - ¿Podría hablar más despacio, por favor?
- Could you repeat this, please? - ¿Podría repetir eso, por favor?
- Me too - Yo también (Use this to say you also agree)
- Me neither - Yo tampoco (Use this to say you also disagree)
- To me, too - A mí también (Use this when responding to liking something)
- To me, neither - A mí tampoco (Use this when responding to disliking something)
- Truth - Neta (Depending on the context, it can also mean honestly or seriously.)
- Is it true? - ¿Es neta?
- Let's practice! - ¡A practicar!
- It's a piece of cake - Es pan comido

- Honestly, I don't believe it. - Neta, no lo creo.
- Don't you think! - ¡A poco no!
- I don't think so - No creo
- What do you think? - ¿Qué opinas?/¿Qué te parece?
- Do you think so? - ¿Tú crees eso?
- I agree. - Estoy de acuerdo.
- I don't agree. - No estoy de acuerdo.
- You know what? ¿Sabes qué?
- Oh, really? - A poco sí (when you have a kind of disbelief with what the other person said)
- On top of that/To top it off - Para colmo
- To make matters worse - Para cagarla aún más
- Don't be stingy! - ¡No seas codo!
- Stop saying stupid things. - Deja de decir tonterías
- Cheat sheet for exam - Acordeón
- Be careful! - ¡Aguas!
- The Beer - La Chela/Cerveza
- Hangover - Estar crudo/cruda
- To be broke [No money] - Estar sin un quinto
- Are you hungry? - ¿Tienes hambre?
- Can you recommend me a restaurant? - ¿Me puede recomendar un restaurante?
- The Waiter/waitress - El Mesero/La Mesera

- What's the wifi password? - ¿Cuál es la clave del wifi?
- Where did I leave the keys? - ¿Dónde dejo las llaves?
- Here you go. - Aquí tiene.

Culture Insights

This section aims to help you understand the context in which the language is used. This chapter requires some research on your part. While all the answers can be found in the back, conducting your own research will enhance your understanding and provide greater insight into the culture.

1. Do you know what the most representative festivities in México are? I'll give you some hints to get you started. After doing some research, you can return and write down your answers.

    - This is a special day in Mexico when everyone goes to the cemetery to leave flowers for their loved ones.

      _____

    - During this celebration, a special altar is set at everyone's house. What is the name of this altar?

      _____

    - For this celebration, Mexico City does a big parade; what can be found in it?

      _____

    - When is Independence Day celebrated in Mexico?

      _____

    - Do you know which country Mexico became independent of?

      _____

    - What can be found on the parade to celebrate this important day?

      _____

    - What is one of the most common foods at a Christmas celebration in Mexico?

- What is the name of the gatherings held in Mexico between the 12th and 24th of December?

- What is a piñata made of?

2. The next questions will give you insight into popular expressions used in everyday conversations.

    - You are invited to a party, and your host says, 'Mi casa es tu casa.' What does this expression mean?

    - You are working on a project your team has yet to start and is due tomorrow. One of your teammates says, 'A darle que es mole de olla.' What does the expression mean?

    - You are talking with your friends, and the little cousin of one of them is making a lot of noise. Your friend shouts at him: 'Ve a ver si ya parió la marrana'. What do you think he means?

    - You ask your friend to help you decide between two things, and he replies, 'No te vayas a quedar como el perro de las dos tortas.' What does he mean?

3. In Mexico, there are many sayings that you will hear a lot. Read the following sayings and try to find their meaning.

- 'El muerto al pozo y el vivo al gozo'

  'The dead to the well and the alive to the joy'

  ___

- 'Olla que mucho hierve, sabor que pierde'

  'A pot that boils a lot loses flavor'

  ___

- 'Le hizo lo que el viento a Juárez'

  'He did what the wind did to Juárez.'

  ___

- 'Este arroz ya se coció'

  'This rice is already cooked.'

  ___

- 'Árbol que crece torcido, su rama nunca endereza'

  'Tree that grows crooked, its branch never straightens.'

  ___

- 'Camarón que se duerme, se lo lleva la corriente'

  'Shrimp that falls asleep, it is carried by the current.'

  ___

4. Mexico is made up of thirty-two states, each with unique characteristics, such as food, places, traditions, etc. Conduct some research and write one or two distinctive features for any five states you choose.

   For example, Mexico City is known for the Zocalo Plaza and the Bellas Artes Palace.

5. Write where the following representative places are in Mexico.

    - La Peña de Bernal

    _____

    - Chichén Itzá

    _____

    - Monte Albán

    _____

    - Teotihuacán

    _____

    - Palenque

    _____

    - Rivera Maya

    _____

    - Pico de Orizaba

    _____

    - Básilica de Santa María de Guadalupe

    _____

    - Ciudad Universitaria

    _____

    - Estado Azteca

    _____

Using these answers, write a sentence about an activity you would like to do at these places if you can visit them.

6. The following questions require you to explore the rich culture of Mexican television, music, literature, and art. I hope you enjoy the process of researching or finding the answers.

    - He is a famous character dressed in a red suit and yellow shorts. He is considered one of the only Mexican superheroes.

      _____

    - He is one of the most recognized singers in Mexico and Latin America, having sold over 100 million copies of his albums worldwide.

      _____

    - She is the most recognized painter in Mexico. Her house is now a museum, and she is well-known worldwide.

      _____

    - This TV program has been on air for 22 years (in 2024). Its host changes from time to time and is aired in the morning.

      _____

    - He is one of the most famous actors in Mexico. He's now known for movies like 'Coda' and 'Instructions Not Included'.

      _____

    - She is one of the most recognized writers in Mexico. Her last name is French; she has lived in Mexico for 82 years.

      _____

      [Note: Answers are on pages 220-223.]

Slang Words

Here are some popular slang words. I encourage you to use them around your friends.

- Cool, Awesome - Chido/Chida, Chingón/Chingona, Padre
- Be careful!/Watch out! - ¡Aguas!
- Really? (express incredulity) - A poco
- No way! (express incredulity) - No manches
- The truth - La Neta
- Job/Work - Chamba/Jale
- What's up? (Informal) - ¿Qué onda?
- Mate/Dude - Güey/Wey
- Close friend/buddy - Cuate/Cuata
- Brother/Sister - Carnal/Carnala
- Young boy/girl - Chavo/Chava
- Something of low quality - Chafa
- Fricking/Damn - Pinche
- I don't care - Equis/Me vale/Me vale queso
- I don't know/Who knows? (Very informal) - Sepa la bola
- Snobby/stuck-up - Fresa
- Someone who is overly frugal with money - Codo/Coda
- See you later! - ¡Ahí nos vidrios!
- Cheers! - ¡Salud!

Do's and Don'ts in Mexico

Do's

- ✔ Do some research on the places you want to visit
- ✔ Try all the food you can, regarding how it can look
- ✔ Ask for suggestions on what to do in the city
- ✔ Use taxis from apps
- ✔ Ask if the salsa is spicy or not
- ✔ Be respectful to elders
- ✔ Attend all parties and gatherings
- ✔ Share the reasons you want to visit the country
- ✔ Exchange money at the airport

Don'ts

- ✖ Don't drink water from the tap
- ✖ Don't cross streets without looking both ways
- ✖ Don't go into restaurants/stores when it's close to its closing/opening hours.
- ✖ Don't go to public toilets without toilet paper.
- ✖ Don't forget to bring a jacket with you
- ✖ Don't talk about stereotypes

Conclusion

Learning a new language is challenging, but you should be proud of your progress. A language encompasses not only words and sentences but also the rich history and culture of many generations. I understand there are difficult days when it may feel like you're not progressing, but these are common experiences for language learners. Don't give up!

If you've found this book helpful in your journey to master Mexican Spanish, please take a moment to share your feedback and leave a review. Your input would be invaluable to others seeking similar resources. Thank you for your support.

Answers

Exercise 1 (Answers)

a) Amigo (friend) - a-**MI**-go

b) Croar (Croak) - cro-**AR**

c) Negativo (Negative) - ne-ga-**TI**-vo

d) Mantequilla (Butter) - man-te-**QUI**-lla

e) Capa (Layer) - **CA**-pa

f) Mago (Magician) - **MA**-go

g) Ducha (Shower) - **DU**-cha

h) Doblado (Folded/Doubled) - do-**BLA**-do

i) Aspiradora (Vacuum) - as-pi-ra-**DO**-ra

j) Cautiverio (Captivity/Imprisonment) - cau-ti-**VE**-rio

k) Aventura (Adventure) - a-ven-**TU**-ra

l) Multiplicar (To multiply) - mul-ti-pli-**CAR**

m) Inundar (To flood/To inundate) - i-nun-**DAR**

n) Comida (Food)- co-**MI**-da

o) Sauna (Sauna) - **SAU**-na

p) Casa (House) - **CA**-sa

q) Bebible (Drinkable) - be-**BI**-ble

r) Castillo (Castle) - cas-**TI**-llo

s) Manicomio (Insane Asylum/Mental institution) - ma-ni-**CO**-mio

t) Punta (Tip/Pointed end/Beach/End/Edge) - **PUN**-ta

u) El Mañana (Tomorrow) - el ma-**ÑA**-na

v) Bengala (Flare) - ben-**GA**-la

w) Carga (Cargo/Load) - **CAR**-ga

x) Sirena (Mermaid) - si-**RE**-na

y) Original (Original) - o-ri-gi-**NAL**

z) Música (Music) - **MÚ**-si-ca

Exercise 2 (Answers)

a) la yegua (the mare) - f

b) el teléfono (the phone) - m

c) la mañana (the morning) - f

d) la música (the music) - f

e) la nieve (the snow) - f

f) el escritorio (the desk) - m

g) el árbol (the tree) - m

h) la guitarra (the guitar) - f

i) la fiesta (the party) - f

j) la piedra (the stone) - f

k) el violin (the violin) - m

l) la nube (the cloud) - f

m) la fotografía (the photography/photograph) - f

n) la mano (the hand) - f

o) el pie (the foot) - m

p) el reloj (the clock) - m

q) el mueble (the furniture) - m

r) la computadora (the computer) - f

Exercise 2.1 (Answers)

a) el candado - los candados (the padlocks)

b) el animal - los animales (the animals)

c) el gato - los gatos (the cats)

d) el árbol - los árboles (the tree)

e) la llave - las llaves (the keys)

f) la casa - las casas (the houses)

g) el espejo - los espejos (the mirrors)

h) la tienda - las tiendas (the shops)

i) la canción - las canciones (the songs)

Exercise 3 (Answers)

a) 32 - treinta y dos

b) 56 - cincuenta y seis

c) 94 - noventa y cuatro

d) 195 - ciento noventa y cinco

e) 396 - trescientos noventa y seis

f) 798 - setecientos noventa y ocho

g) 1.132 - mil ciento treinta y dos

h) 4.341 - cuatro mil trescientos cuarenta y uno

i) 9.832 - nueve mil ochocientos treinta y dos

j) 10.341 - diez mil trescientos cuarenta y uno

k) 51.556 - cincuenta y uno mil quinientos cincuenta y seis

l) 72.761 - setenta y dos mil setecientos sesenta y uno

m) 112.445 - ciento doce mil cuatrocientos cuarenta y cinco

n) 556.789 - quinientos cincuenta y seis mil setecientos ochenta y nueve

o) 890.987 - ochocientos noventa mil novecientos ochenta y siete

p) 1.000.000 - un millón

q) 1.000.000.000 - mil millones/millardo

r) 1.000.000.000.000 - un billón

Exercise 3.1 (Answers)

a) 12th - décimosegundo

b) 25th - vigésimo quinto

c) 34th - trigésimo cuarto

d) 49th - cuadragésimo noveno

e) 55th - quincuagésimo quinto

f) 67th - sexagésimo séptimo

g) 78th - septuagésimo octavo

h) 84th - octogésimo cuarto

i) 99th - nonagésimo noveno

Exercise 4 (Answers)

1) What is the subject pronoun for 'You' (Informal)?

   d) Tú

2) What is the subject pronoun for 'You all'?

   d) Ustedes

3) What is the subject pronoun for 'She'?

   c) Ella

4) What is the subject pronoun for 'We' (all women)?

   d) Nosotras

5) What is the subject pronoun for 'They' (Mixed gender)?

   a) Ellos

Exercise 4.1 (Answers)

1) What is the function of the adjective?

   a) **Modify or describe nouns and pronouns**

2) In Spanish, where do adjectives of size, shape, color, and personality usually go in a sentence?

   b) **After the noun**

3) In Spanish, where do adjectives of quantity or number usually go in a sentence?

   b) **Before the noun**

4) What is the masculine form for 'this' in Spanish?

   c) **Este**

5) What is the feminine form for 'those' when referring to objects or people near you?

d) **Esas**

6) What is the masculine form for 'those' when referring to objects or people far from you?

   c) **Aquellos**

7) What is the masculine form for 'mine' in Spanish?

   c) **Mío**

Exercise 4.2 (Answers)

1) Escondió el vestido **en** el closet. (She hid the dress **in** the closet.)

   b) **en**

2) Lo enviaré **por** correo postal. (I will send it **through** postal mail.)

   a) **por**

3) Este regalo lo compré **para** ti. (I bought this gift **for** you.)

   b) **para**

4) Se resfrió **por** culpa del frío. (He caught a cold **because** of the cold.)

   a) **por**

5) Escuché música **durante** el viaje. (I listened to music **during** the trip.)

   c) **durante**

Exercise 5 (Answers)

Verb: Cantar (To sing)

- I sing - Yo canto
- You sing - Tú cantas
- He sings - Él canta

- We sing - Nosotros/Nosotras <u>cantamos</u>
- They sing - Ellos/Ellas <u>cantan</u>

Verb: Leer (To read)

- I read - Yo <u>leo</u>
- You read - Tú <u>lees</u>
- He reads - Él <u>lee</u>
- We read - Nosotros/Nosotras <u>leemos</u>
- They read - Ellos/Ellas <u>leen</u>

Verb: Escribir (To write)

- I write - Yo <u>escribo</u>
- You write - Tú <u>escribes</u>
- He writes - Él <u>escribe</u>
- We write - Nosotros/Nosotras <u>escribimos</u>
- They write - Ellos/Ellas <u>escriben</u>

Here is a list of additional regular infinitive verbs for you to practice at your convenience. These verbs encompass various actions and are helpful in everyday conversations.

-ar verbs

Abandonar - To abandon

Abrazar - To hug

Averiguar - To find out

Ayudar - To help

Bailar - To dance

Bañar - To bathe

Caminar - To walk

Causar - To cause

Cocinar - To cook

Comprar - To buy

Cuidar - To take care

Degustar - To taste

Enviar - To send

Escuchar - To listen

Esperar - To wait / To hope

Estudiar - To study

Ganar - To win / To earn

Limpiar - To clean

Llamar - To call

Llegar - To arrive

Llevar - To carry / To wear

Luchar - To fight

Mirar - To look / To watch

Nadar - To swim

Peinar - To comb

Preguntar - To ask (is used when you want to ask a question.)

Tomar - To take / To drink

Trabajar - To work

Visitar - To visit

-er verbs

Aparecer - To appear

Aprender - To learn

Barrer - To sweep

Beber - To drink

Comprender - To understand

Correr - To run

Coser - To sew

Creer - To believe

Deber - To owe / To must

Defender - To depend

Esconder - To hide

Ofender - To offend

Ofrecer - To offer

Prometer - To promise

Responder - To respond

Romper - To break

Sorprender - To surprise

Temer - To fear

Vender - To sell

-ir verbs

Abrir - To open

Admitir - To admit

Asistir - To attend

Compartir - To share

Cumplir - To fulfill/ To turn or be a certain age

Decidir - To decide

Describir - To describe

Descubrir - To discover

Discutir - To argue

Discutir - To discuss / To argue

Dividir- To split / To divide

Existir - To exist

Imprimir - To print

Insistir - To insist

Omitir - To omit

Partir - To split / To depart

Pedir - To ask (is used when you want to obtain something from someone; it can be borrowed or given entirely.)

Permitir - To allow / To permit

Persuadir - To persuade

Recibir - To receive

Repetir - To repeat

Subir - To go up/ To raise / To upload

Unir - To unite / To join

Exercise 5.1 (Answers)

- Comer (to eat) - Comiendo (Eating)
- Hablar (to speak) - Hablando (Speaking)
- Ir (to go) - Yendo (Going)
- Leer (to read) - Leyendo (Reading)
- Vivir (to live) - Viviendo (Living)

Exercise 5.2 (Answers)

- Hablar (to speak) - Hablado (Spoken)
- Comer (to eat) - Comido (Eaten)
- Vivir (to live) - Vivido (Lived)
- Escribir (to write) - Escrito (Written)
- Abrir (to open) - Abierto (open)

Exercise 5.3 (Answers)

Verb: Levantarse (to get up)

- I get up - Yo me levanto
- You get up - Tú te levantas
- He gets up - Él se levanta
- We get up - Nosotros/Nosotras nos levantamos

- They get up - Ellos/Ellas se <u>levantan</u>

Verb: Lavarse (to wash oneself)

- I wash - Yo me <u>lavo</u>
- You wash - Tú te <u>lavas</u>
- He washes - Él se <u>lava</u>
- We wash - Nosotros/Nosotras nos <u>lavamos</u>
- They wash - Ellos/Ellas se <u>lavan</u>

Verb: Vestirse (to get dressed)

- I get dressed - Yo me <u>visto</u>
- You get dressed - Tú te <u>vistes</u>
- He gets dressed - Él se <u>viste</u>
- We get dressed - Nosotros/Nosotras nos <u>vestimos</u>
- They get dressed - Ellos/Ellas se <u>visten</u>

Exercise 5.4 (Answers)

- <u>Me</u> levanto temprano. (I get up early.)
- <u>Nos</u> vestimos rápido. (We get dressed quickly.)
- <u>Se</u> acuesta a las diez. (He/She goes to bed at ten.)
- <u>Se</u> despiertan tarde. (They wake up late.)
- <u>Te</u> lavas las manos. (You wash your hands.)

Exercise 5.5 (Answers)

- Nosotros siempre comemos juntos el domingo. (We always eat together on Sunday.)

- Marta habla español muy bien. (Marta speaks Spanish very well.)
- El profesor habla muy rápido. (The teacher speaks very fast.)
- Nosotros vivimos en una casa grande. (We live in a big house.)

Culture Insights (Answers)

1. The most representative festivities in México.

    - This special day in Mexico is when everyone goes to the cemetery to leave flowers for their loved ones. **_Día de los Muertos_**

    - During this celebration, a special altar is set at everyone's house. What is the name of this altar? **_Ofrenda_**

    - For this celebration, Mexico City does a big parade; what can be found in it? **_Big walking skeletons_**

    - When is Independence Day celebrated in Mexico? **_September 16th_**

    - Do you know which country Mexico became independent of? **_Spain_**

    - What can be found on the parade to celebrate this important day? **_A military show_**

    - What is one of Mexico's most common foods at a Christmas celebration? **_Turkey_**

    - What is the name of the gatherings held in Mexico between the 12th and 24th of December? **_Posadas_**

    - What is a piñata made of? **_Cardboard_**

2. Popular expressions that are used in everyday conversations.

    - You are invited to a party, and your host says, 'Mi casa es tu casa.' What does this expression mean?

        It means you can feel comfortable at their house as much as if it were yours.

    - You are working on a project your team has yet to start and is due tomorrow. One of your teammates says, 'A darle que es mole de olla.' What does the expression mean?

It means you must hurry to start doing something that will take a while.

- You are talking with your friends, and the little cousin of one of them is making a lot of noise. Your friend shouts at him: 'Ve a ver si ya parió la marrana'. What do you think he means?

It means that he should go somewhere else.

- You ask your friend to help you decide between two things, and he replies, 'No te vayas a quedar como el perro de las dos tortas.' What does he mean?

It refers to a story where a dog tries to eat too much and, in the end, doesn't get any of it.

3. Mexican sayings that you will hear a lot.

    - 'El muerto al pozo y el vivo al gozo'

      'The dead to the well and the alive to the joy'

      Life keeps going, and you should, as well.

    - 'Olla que mucho hierve, sabor que pierde'

      'A pot that boils a lot loses flavor'

      You should not delay solving problems or some matters.

    - 'Le hizo lo que el viento a Juárez'

      'He did what the wind did to Juárez.'

      Something didn't have any effect.

    - 'Este arroz ya se coció'

      'This rice is already cooked.'

      Something (a matter) is over.

    - 'Árbol que crece torcido, su rama nunca endereza'

'Tree that grows crooked, its branch never straightens.'

Someone can't change the way they were educated/the way they grew up.

- 'Camarón que se duerme, se lo lleva la corriente'

'Shrimp that falls asleep is carried by the current.'

It advises against being lazy and not paying attention to what is happening around you.

5. The location of the representative places in Mexico.

    - La Peña de Bernal **_Querétaro_**

    - Chichén Itzá **_Mérida_**

    - Monte Albán **_Oaxaca_**

    - Teotihuacán **_Mexico City_**

    - Palenque **_Chiapas_**

    - Rivera Maya **_Quintana Roo_**

    - Pico de Orizaba **_Veracruz_**

    - Básilica de Santa María de Guadalupe **_Mexico City_**

    - Ciudad Universitaria **_Mexico City_**

    - Estado Azteca **_Mexico City_**

6. The rich culture of Mexican television, music, literature, and art.

    - He is a famous character dressed in a red suit and yellow shorts. He is considered one of the only Mexican superheroes.

    Chapulín Colorado

    - He is one of the most recognized singers in Mexico and Latin America, having sold over 100 million copies of his albums worldwide.

Juan Gabriel

- She is the most recognized painter in Mexico. Her house is now a museum, and she is well-known worldwide.

Frida Kahlo

- This TV program has been on air for 22 years (in 2024). Its host changes from time to time and is aired in the morning.

Hoy

- He is one of the most famous actors in Mexico. He's now known for movies like 'Coda' and 'Instructions Not Included'.

Eugenio Derbez

- She is one of the most recognized writers in Mexico. Her last name is French; she has lived in Mexico for 82 years.

Elena Poniatowska

References

- *Gramática y Ortografía Básicas de la Lengua Española, RAE*. (n.d.). RAE.

- *Nueva Gramática de la Lengua Española, RAE*. (n.d.). RAE.

- Franzen, S. (2024, July 19). The Spanish Alphabet - Spelling and pronunciation. *Let's Speak Spanish*. https://letsspeakspanish.com/blog/spanish-alphabet/

- Miguel. (2018, September 27). *The Ultimate Guide to Spanish Pronunciation (with Audio and Video!) – Spanish for Your Job*. https://spanishforyourjob.com/pronunciation/

- The Language School. (2016, December 9). *Pronunciation - Y and LL - Part 1: México* [Video]. YouTube. https://www.youtube.com/watch?v=6XOS6QDwV3M

- Put, O. (2021, April 30). *A Beginner's guide to Spanish syllables*. Homeschool Spanish Academy. https://www.spanish.academy/blog/a-beginners-guide-to-spanish-syllables/

- Señor Jordan. (2022, February 13). *How to know if a Noun is Masculine or Feminine Spanish (Revised 2022)* [Video]. YouTube. https://www.youtube.com/watch?v=wvMY7wYYOU0

- *Spanish Plurals - free online Spanish lessons*. (n.d.). https://www.thespanishexperiment.com/learn-spanish/plurals

- Sanchez, D., & Sanchez, D. (2023, April 7). Spanish Plural Words 101: Making nouns plural in Spanish. *Tell Me In Spanish*. https://www.tellmeinspanish.com/grammar/spanish-plural-nouns/

- Blacklingual. (2022, August 11). *Difference between el and la in Spanish 😊 How to say the & a in Spanish* [Video]. YouTube. https://www.youtube.com/watch?v=ZQI1jqTqw6E

- Blacklingual. (2022b, August 15). *Rules for el and la in Spanish 😊* [Video]. YouTube. https://www.youtube.com/watch?v=I8h2LmWafwk

- Blacklingual. (2021, May 20). *How to count to over a million in spanish 🤖 Hundreds, thousands, millions, and billions in Spanish* [Video]. YouTube. https://www.youtube.com/watch?v=vBe-TurndhA
- Sanchez, D., & Sanchez, D. (2024, July 13). How to tell time in Spanish: Formula, rules & examples. *Tell Me In Spanish.* https://www.tellmeinspanish.com/grammar/how-to-tell-time-in-spanish/#how_to_add_minutes
- Blacklingual. (2021b, September 11). *The calendar in Spanish 📅 how to say dates in Spanish* [Video]. YouTube. https://www.youtube.com/watch?v=w3OPPJb9sg0
- Mexico, N. (2024, May 1). *Object pronouns in Spanish — Na'Atik Language & Culture Institute.* Na'atik Language & Culture Institute. https://naatikmexico.org/blog/object-pronouns-in-spanish
- Galavitz, R., & Galavitz, R. (2024, September 19). *100+ most common Spanish adjectives (And How to use them!) - Rosetta Stone.* Rosetta Stone. https://blog.rosettastone.com/most-common-spanish-adjectives/
- *Learn and practise Spanish grammar.* (n.d.). https://espanol.lingolia.com/en/grammar
- Monroy, M. (2023, April 26). A nifty list of 46 Spanish prepositions: Place, relation, time. *Berlitz.* https://www.berlitz.com/blog/spanish-prepositions-list
- SpanishPod101.com. (2024, October 7). *The Ultimate guide to Spanish tenses - SpanishPod101.com blog.* SpanishPod101.com Blog. https://www.spanishpod101.com/blog/2021/07/08/spanish-tenses/
- Mykhalevych, N. (2024, October 3). Irregular Spanish Verbs & Their Conjugation Charts. *Language learning with Preply Blog.* https://preply.com/en/blog/irregular-spanish-verbs/
- Serpas, T. (2022, November 1). *Spanish stem changing verbs (+ practice and cheatsheet).* Spanish With Tati. https://spanishwithtati.com/conjugate-spanish-irregular-verbs/

- Fajkus, M. M. (2021, February 9). *Spanish gerunds: the ultimate guide to the progressive tenses.* Homeschool Spanish Academy. https://www.spanish.academy/blog/spanish-gerunds-the-ultimate-guide-to-the-progressive-tenses/#:~:text=In%20simple%20terms%2C%20the%20gerund,I%20am%20eating%20breakfast

- *How to use past participles in Spanish?* (n.d.). https://mangolanguages.com/resources/learn/grammar/spanish/how-to-use-past-participles-in-spanish

- Adrian. (2024, June 27). *Spanish sentence structure: The Big 6 explained.* BaseLang. https://baselang.com/blog/basic-grammar/spanish-sentence-structure/?utm_source=youtube&utm_medium=youtube-channel&utm_campaign=youtube-machine&utm_content=sentence-structure&utm_term=youtube-viewers

- Sanchez, D., & Sanchez, D. (2023b, August 12). Question Words in Spanish: 8 key Interrogative Words. *Tell Me In Spanish.* https://www.tellmeinspanish.com/vocab/spanish-question-words/#Qui%C3%A9n-Who

- Put, O. (2021b, July 16). *A simple guide to Spanish sentence structure and order.* Homeschool Spanish Academy. https://www.spanish.academy/blog/a-simple-guide-to-spanish-sentences-and-their-structure/

- Learn Spanish with SpanishPod101.com. (2020, April 9). *Essential restaurant phrases in Mexican Spanish* [Video]. YouTube. https://www.youtube.com/watch?v=oRuhw9eqCcY

- Blakney, R. (2022, April 26). *Mexican slang Terms.* Live Lingua. https://www.livelingua.com/blog/mexican-slang-terms/